THE ONEIRONAUT
Ø2

Sheri-D Wilson

Write Bloody Publishing

writebloody.com

First edition.
ISBN: 978-1-7781626-3-3

Cover Design: Henry Sene Yee
Interior Layout: Michal Kozlowski
Editor: Micheline Maylor
Author Photo: Kimberley French

Write Bloody North, Canada
Support Independent Presses
writebloodynorth.ca

Thank you to the Canada Council, the Alberta Foundation for the Arts, and the Calgary Spoken Word Society.

For the children of the water
who learned to swim
in abyssal realms

THE ONEIRONAUT
Ø2

Contents

"I've always had access to other worlds.
We all do because we dream."
– Leonora Carrington

Meanwhile

On the zenith of a plateau
atop a very tall sea stack,
hewn by nature
out of labradorite stone,

seven women known
as the Willows of Sweven,
are deep in ceremony.

Waves crash all around
the solitary sentinel rising
out of a boundless sea.

They are. They are nought.

Chanting marvellously, wearing identical
midnight blue persona masks,
with spirals of galaxies vivified
over their 3rd eyes.

It is. It is nought.

A night sky fused in phoenix.
The Willows of Sweven, clad in red robes
radiate around an astronomical firebowl
which glows orange and red and ember gold
omphaloi.

Sparks fill the air. Quasi-sun solar flare. Inferno.

Wisps of sandalwood, cedar and juniper – swirl
omnisciently from the spire carrying a missive
to the sentient beings. It ascends higher,
this clairvoyant billow of seeing,
to summon the serpent

and aid them on their quest.

Nine giant eagles circle the summit
as the Willows reorder themselves, stars zing
across the night sky. Streaks of light, of life.

The Willows shed their cloaks, ecdysis into beauty,
they turn to salt, pure as well water.

<<<<<<<*Rain gets blitzed on bourbon to avoid*
the changes she must make, no mistake, to survive>>>>>>>

The Willows breathe the fumes
of numinous spirits – which awakens their masks –
they metamorphose into a prismatic thunder of crows.

Transmundane, they summon Aves chaos,
hallooing chromatic plumes in fiery hues.
The Willows dance light-footed without any shoes, in ebony
indigo.

Flickering. Ineffable sparks shoot from their crowns
eudaimonic.

Parados

ᛏᛟ ᛞᛟ ᛟᚱ ᛞᛁᛖ ᛏᛟ ᛒᛖ ᚠᚾᛞ ᛚᛖᛏ ᛒᛖ

Speaking Crow in Chorus
The Willows Recap the Key
ᛊᛈᛁᚱᛁᛏ ᚲᚺᚨᛜᛖ

(All)
Williwaw. We amplify higher
frequencies with urgency.

Previously,
in The Oneironaut Ø1—

The DOD, Department of Dreams,
requires all citizens of X-City
to take a MetaNoia pill everyday,
which stops them from dreaming.

Rain, a scientist living in X-City
hears the call of the Serpent,
and is pinged awake – awake,
she stops taking her pill.

By decree, there will be no reverie.
ᛞᚱᛖᛗ ᛊᛈᛖᛚᛚ

This is menticide,
DOD brain control weaponry.

Mistrust has run roughshod
over the citizens of X-City,
not to speak of division, despair
and hopelessness, ahhhhh.

Unbeknownst to Rain
she's become a nebulous rebel,
who has unlocked the door
to the forbidden. Ahhhhh.

She abruptly quits her job
and soon stumbles into a prohibited
bookshop, where she chances upon
a SciNow article entitled, 'The Oneironaut.'

For the first time in her life, she glimpses
at the world of possibility. PING!
Lights on – mind zips off.

Rain leaves X-City in search
of the illusive Oneironaut. She finds Lily,
far off-grid behind a bulwark firewall
in a hidden Elysium called Sweven.

Lily lives among
other dissident dreamers,
ahhhhh, that's us, the Willows.

By decree, there will be no reverie.
ᛞᚱᛖᛗ ᛊᛈᛖᛚᛚ

Rain must return to X-City
for reasons to be revealed shortly.
All-chaos erupts.
PING!

Currently,
the DOD, subdivision of The Bureau,
have discovered Rain's transgressions,
and issued an all-points APB dragnet
for her capture and arrest.

If they catch her, they catch us.
If they catch us, they catch the Serpent.
If they catch the Ouroboros, it will end
all dwimmer and dream healing.

Parallelly,
Rain, unable to face
the unresolved trauma of subjugation
is getting pissed on Shadow
Market bourbon.

ᚹᛖ ᚲᚨᛚᛚ ᛊᚾᚨᚲᛖ ᚨᚾᛞ ᚱᚨᛁᚾ ᚾᛟᚹ

(Jet)
All worlds are unfolding into one
liminality – real into unreal
surreality and vice versa.

Please be advised, the Ovoid Pearl
has been compromised,
our frequencies jammed.

The gold ray has crystallized.
We've engaged Gauge, Rain's
star-mate to help navigate
tempestuous waters.

PING!

THE BUREAU
DEPARTMENT OF DREAMS
SECURITY INTELLIGENCE REPORT
CODE RED

File: 210178MS5E
Date/Time: Non-Subjunctive Future Escalating
Subject: Rain (ID # 220 455 816)

VIOLATION REPORT:
Subject Quit job @ Internal Sub-unit.
Discontinued MetaNoia – Conclusive.
Shoplifted Uncatalogued Item (Bookstore).
Surveilled – Out Past-Curfew (Shadow Market).

Rented a Vehicle (Rent-a-Ruin). No Permit or Clearance.
Left X-City Limits.
Suspected Association w/ Dissidents.
~~Disappeared into thin air. Fell off-grid.~~

Returned to X-City.
Suspected Nox Chieftain Super Dreamer.
Conveying False Information.

Circumvented: Tracking Surveillance, Security
Screening Checkpoints, Probs & Drones,
Roadblocks & Unit Patrols.

OFFICIAL STATUS:
Dangerous Person Alert.

RECOMMENDATION:
Apprehend Alive.

Panopticon Surveillance # 220 002 336 – The Perp's Mother.

Inside The Bureau.

Dr. Lester Maggott, Director, Department of Dreams, sits behind a palatial desk devoid of doodads, except for a gold-plated plaque inscribed with his namesake.

He's squeaky clean on the outside, with meticulous hair perfectly coiffed to appear stylishly effortless, yet he's a mannequin-made virtue-signaler.

Lester's not an autocrat fascist stereotype, no, more inconspicuous, sympathetic to the ordinary person. Yet there's something suspiciously awry about his flawlessness. Looks deceive, he's fiendish to the core.

He doesn't sport a tooth-brush mustache, but he's definitely the epitome of a treacherous dictator.

The pièce de resistance concerning his anti-wacky style are his frameless status quo bio-spectacles, innocuous yet deadly.

Maggott barks orders machine-gun-style at Shelly, who's a dead ringer for Igor the lackey, except this humble-brag wears a prig-of-prim pearls. Shelly's dressed on-trend in a sleek khaki jumpsuit, with her pants neatly tucked into high leather boots.

She's akin to a clipped toady in an absurdist play, because as she responds to Maggot her feet continue to run on the spot. Shelly is simultaneously mobile and stationary at the same time, as if continuously riding a bureaucratic exercise bike.

Irritated by her antsy worminess, Maggott screams, "Shelly! Stand still! Are you listening? I want a full dossier of this miscreant # 220 455 816 on my desk by noon.

I want to know where she goes, who she knows, every place she's ever gone, authorised and not. We need every detail of her existence, every vice and quirk – affiliation and communication.

Delve deep! I want to see a complete report of her financial information – down to every transaction. It's incumbent on us to uncover all transgressions and indiscretions. This includes a complete history of her medical files and a comprehensive forensic algorithm scan. I want to know what makes her tick before the time bomb reaches it's final tock!"

"Okay. Okay, boss."

"And, up the torture levels of # 799."

Rain's Data Log

Private Notes XXIV – Unravelling Unconsciousness

edge

W d

some

where

be

tween

cognitive

dissonance and quantum

uncertainty

betwixt

hexadecimal

confusion

and personal

epistemology, is me,

drunk as a skunk – *or skunked*

as a drunk, even my Merrow

is sloshed – she's trying

to slide off my hand.

Why am I suddenly drinking?

My mind's wiving & weaving,

just fell off

the page

onto the grey rug, oh no,

I'm a gyrating coin, no

I'm a b-girl stuck-in a permanent headspin.

Whoa, dizzy spell. Sip. Sip.

Drinking's the only way to catch
my breath,
or a <•) (((((-< .

This apartment's so boring it fades
into its own dull existence. Why didn't I notice it
before? Note to sterile self: my countertops
are always too clean. Sip. Sip.

How many worlds exist at once?

It looks like no one lives here. *They don't.*

I'm axiomatically hooped, deadlocked
in an infinite loop
of chaos, *a 404 error,*

caught in an algorithmic roundabout
of terror – a helical maze,

a fisheye gaze.

<<<<<<<[fish.exe fatal error]>>>>>>>
Gotta scrub the bug.

My entire life's been a lie. Don't know
who I am anymore.   Sip.

What would my brother do
if he was me, if he was here to help me.
Why did she give him up?
Give up on him—

I could spill oil on this ugly coffee table
and it wouldn't even bat an eye. It might even
welcome something as hideous as itself.
Why am I an ugly coffee table?

No, the only thing that's real is this prohibited
bottle of Shadow Market bourbon.
"Huzzzah."
I'll sip this neurostimulating transcendental
simulating amber elixir véridique
until my life makes sense again.

Sip.   Sip.   Sip.

I'm chasing my own
<•) (((((-<

or maybe my own <•) (((((-<

is chasing me.

Maybe inebriation will get closer to having
a ~~dream~~ fish.

I could buy a tablecloth. That picture of Maggott is
really starting to eat at me. Time to toss it.
Later. Sip. Sip.
At least I have a lowball glass.

No, every nanosecond I remain ichthyoidal-less
the possibility of a fish latch
becomes more illusive, slipperier
than silicone spaghetti.

Trying to debone an oily <•) (((((-<

slimy code for forget it, finding a cipher, nil.
Sip.

At first there was a burning
sensation. Now, it's going down smooth.

∵ ∴ Deduction ∴ ∵
I'm officially wasted – covertly fish sauced.

The DOD's steely digits are tightening
around my neck – squeezing my eyes out
of their sockets,

we're closed circuit shivil-llians,
spies rrrrrrr ev-ery-where,

can't trushst anyone,

security patrols
eyelet knotholes. *Darknet!*

I am I am not

A fish Out of water

Who is itself Out of water

I never met A Metafish
I didn't like.

Living in a palindromic number,
losing my inhibishu

n

n

n

n

n

n

s n
n n
n

RINGRING.
My burner! "Shite!"
Must be Gauge.

Better straighten up my lace-shs! He's never seen me drunk.

"Hello— [*c=speed of light in a vacuum*]

yup everything's—

no, just a little loaded—

on Overclocker—

at the Shadow Market—no,

just a little tipsy—

no, dodged the bullet-cams—

wearing a mask—but we shouldn't

be talking about this—

even on contraband burners.

Yeah—no

me too— *[Δt]*

call you tomorrow— "

CLICK.

Notebook of LM

Entry X – Tumbling Down a Flight of Stares

Back at Sweven. Nightfall. I don't want to,
but I have to face the PTSD I've suffered since
Che was taken from me.

It's time to draw down the stairs and eradicate
the fiends that are living above me in the attic.
Yes, it's time for me to climb the stairs and enter,
katabasis.

Sunlight breaks through the glass wall and spills
into the sunroom, a bard's message.

Sigh of dread, guess I'm going to do this, yes,
it's time to return to the mortal tomb above
our living room.

Geckos love sunlight and they all scurry to get
the best spot as usual they make me laugh inside
my being.

Haven't entered the loft since the DOD fish attack
that killed Che and stripped me of my Oneironaut
powers.

The Geckos create the coat of the Taliesin on every
surface of the sunroom, which grants me a moment
of lyricism, before

my dolor is once again eclipsed by anvil thoughts.
The DOD rendered me naut-less, yes, they took my
Triquetra knot. Ever since then my fishes have been
in a twist.

Just thinking about it guts me, it guts me, besieged

by a frisson of fear, it sears my nerves. I remember that Grim Reaper night when everything dear was taken from me. I'm glad I have creatures to remind me to live. They need me as I need them, to live. The entire creep of Geckos is already fast asleep, basking in a ballad of ultraviolet light. I hear harps.

The last of my O-naut might be entombed by the soul snatchers up there still. That Letifer of Martifer's have haunted us with the slashes of their lethal scythes ever since.

Nuance whistles from the other room and calls Lily. *WHISTLE! LILY!*

I reply with the long-drawn transcendental whistle he likes so much and call, Nuance, come here my flair feathered friend, thanks for breaking my distrait spell.

He flies in, an iridescent trail follows him as well as a light trace of twinkling pons. His eyes are bugging out slightly, which tells me he knows something obscura is afoot. Nevertheless,

he lands on my shoulder with a light bump, which is meant to nudge me into spilling. So, I spill—

Honeybird, I know you and the critter crew are highly sensitive to paranormal activity because you wake-up from your sleep when the dark forces wail above us.

SQUAWK! We do. We are. We have. We will. What's up? I know, sometimes their noises shake the entire Clove awake. The Geckos freak out. Wreak havoc.

Well, it's time to end this tyranny.

SQUAWK! Yes, it's time. It's time! *TRILL!* For what?
What is it time for? What are we doing here?
It's time I either retrieve my Oneironaut, which is living
aloft, or I lose myself trying.

SQUAWK! Birds of a feather must stick together.
Cowards die many times before they eventually
kick the bucket. The valiant only taste death once,
so fluckit. *FLUCKIT!*

O Barnacles! That's exactly what I'm afraid of.
And by the way, nice rewrite. Sometimes I'm not
certain who reveres whom more. He flies and lands
on the singing bowl. His toenails *PING* it.

SQUAWK! We'll all pop our crocs one day, Lily.
Pop our crocs *LET'S POP OUR CROCS* Nukey
clicks his abalone beak against the crystal singing
bowl *PING. PING. PING.*

My sweat glands over-salivate, just thinking about it.
O Shellfish! I'm suffering hard-core hyper-hidrosis,
trying to defy my fear of the attic sky.

SQUAWK! You got this, Lily. You got this.

Thank you, Nuance. Thank you.

SQUAWK! Face your fear. And take your fizgig
spear up there too! *SQUAWK!*

Okay I got it. And I can't forget the attic key.

<<<<<<<you got this, Lily>>>>>>>

Scared stiff. I lower the ladder.

SQUAWK! Creepy. Squeaky.

Sshh. I pull down the rope, axis mundi, double
helix and slowly climb the loft ladder, one DNA
rung at a time.

Nuance murmurs, I'm with you, Lily. *TRILL
TRILLTRILL*!

... the cosmic serpent staircase of clever fools.

TRILLTRILL! Amathia. Intelligent stupidity.
Nigh cowards. It's broken lucidity.

I can't breathe, ascending towards Erebos, up,
up, until I reach the last rung

of paradox, which connects and separates us
all at once, the verso trapdoor, tears of fear well.
I can't see, my vision is opaque.

Turn the key, *CLICK!* Mercury shoots up my spine.
I open the hatch, inch sliver-by-sliver. Whisper aft
to Nuance, can you hear me, are you still there?

TRILL! That creak sounds more like a screech.
Even the hatch is horrified to be opened. Even it's
aghast at what it imagines might lie beyond itself.
ITSELF! ITSELF!

I slowly climb inside the attic chamber, shivved by
a serrated chill – a cryogenic deathification slashes
into me,

the stench of pending death swings me half-world-
wise, triggers paranormal knives caught in the wake
of the rattle, clattering inside the echo of the ossuary.

Winded, I eek out, I'm here—ready—or—not—
said as a warning, likely heard as a bluff. It's really
flawed fakery. I've never been great at feigning
confidence.

Gag! The smell of dead flesh lodges in my throat.
I hack up a phantom oyster, an invisible hairball.

The attic's exactly as I left it, when Che left me, or
was taken. I ran for my life. *CRACK* crystalline and cold,
beyond post-mortem, freeze.

My father's voice taunts me, it re-haunts me. Every
time I feel terror-stricken, I hear childhood re-runs
in my head,

him yelling, "you think you're something special
'cause you're an Oneironaut, well you're not unique.
And wipe that smile off your face before I wipe it
off for you."

Each fear bead breeds multitudes of others – things
that have happened, things that haven't – a literal
domino flow of self-destruction.

A lethal wind whizzes through my heart. The attic
walls ice and a stridulous high-pitched sound wails.
It wails out beyond caterwaul.

CRACK of ice. O Killing Grounds!

Massive bodkin needles, saw-toothed icicles, pierce the room from all angles. Closing in on us – there's... nowhere to escape.

Nuance grips his claws into my shoulder as we're bombarded by giant spear-like ice spikes, jutting, stabbing in through the ceiling and walls, until the attic's a veritable Iron Maiden!

Nukey screams, we're trapped in a cage of enraged mortality. He digs his claws into my shoulderblade. *SQUAWK!*

Rain's Data Log
Private Notes XXV – Club Banality

Ahhhhh, sink into the cloud that is my couch,
yeah, sync, become one with the couch cloud.

Exhausted, I might actually sleep. *Mwahahaha*!

Catch a little shit-faced shuteye, ZZZZZZZZZ,
somnium delirium, brainslide headfirst into Sim

VR nightlife. Oh yeah, that night in the MetaVerse
dimension – a complete blend of immersception.
Oh yeah, the night I met Gauge, I was—

> *fully shroomed, I strapped on my headset & slid*
> *inside the underground VR venue without a key,*
> *instantly, somehow,*
>
> *I managed to skip the back-alley 3rd degree & landed*
> *dead centre in an atmospheric spectacle – smackdab*
> *in the middle of the main dance floor in Club Banality,*
>
> *& I was mid-dance-move, rapt in a full windmill*
> *B-girl twirl, peaking in a sim-swing swirl – dancing*
> *the magic forward – forward to magic dancing.*
>
> *IRL the full moon was wilder than the boon, more howl*
> *in my spirit than usual. But I don't believe in that stuff.*
> *Re: Zoom—*
>
> *Club Banality's poppin' in full psilocybin plumes*
> *& I'm engaged in three realities at once.*
>
> *I'm high as Olympus Mons on Mars in two,*
> *& I've got one foot on solid ground in the other.*

Unreal in high-rez BOOMWHIZBOOM groove,
hot luminesce, glow stick phosphorescence, hard-
hitting house BOOMWHIZBOOM whiz-kid
DJ Strobe at the helm,

of the avatars. Our moves electric blue multisonic
in a sea of stroboscopic special effects, encircling
us in a mysterium of joyance,

a nexus of pixel peep roar, pumped with passion,
we soar, speak euphoria in a lost twilight language
with advanced apperception,

walls plastered with proto-graffiti, thrum bassline
drum, low drone BOOMWHIZBOOM everything
melding together—

trippin' & flippin' between twistin'
void self & absolute le flash self

peaking on shrooms in total immersion
in bit-rot rave aesthetic, spark charged.

The other avatar revellers are shooting stars,
chrysalis bio-bots, flipping from one form
to another with complete fluidity, immersed
inside a holo-trace, dancing with ecstatic flow
when—

My Ophiuchi catches the eye of another η *Ophiuchi.*

Never met anyone online whose name synergized
with mine, whose stars harmonized with mine.
Quantum leap.

Never believed in kismet, 6th sense, déjà vu, or fate,
none of that jabberwocky malarkey.

But this was an undefinable heart piercing CLICK.
I mouthed, 'Rain,' as η *Ophiuchi signed, 'Gauge.'*

Rain / Ophiuchi – Gauge/ η *Ophiuchi.*

We twigged inside each other's silent messages.

Don't know if I cared if Gauge was his real name.
Don't know why I gave him mine. We just—
CLICKED *as human beings who are*
not human beings.

We slid inside each other's marvelous whimsy,
inside a crazy kind of destiny. There was no why or how.
I slid inside his photorealistic puma crow-personae, dark
as a rolling storm, rom baro, zingaro – and it was a rush,

of fear blood-rage that blazed inside me. I was alive.
Wild inside his histrionic eyes, fever grew feral
as we rewilded the wilderness.

Instinctively, he twirled his catamount tail, spark
plug ZZZZZZ *– another crazy-rush inside me,*
a flamethrower's pyroshadow, haptic

feedback on all three levels, omni-dimensional
arousal,

panoptic in every realm, the stars of our avatars
aligned & I was powerless to disengage,

we were on an emotional rampage– big cats freed

from their cage – bodies rolling feline. We slipped
into a sidebar pod to pursue the real in the un &
the un in the real to reveal galaxies beyond
ourselves,

tingling, intermingling, we were intertwining a time
out of time in perfect time – mist sprayed over us
as we twisted our minds into an endless knot,

whispering eternal – helpless to resist,
all, each, every, any, absolute – oui, oui, oui,

I could have been anyone, in that moment,
but all I wanted was to be myself, for once,

the earth dropped away
and we were lost in the infinite,

free to traverse the ultimate universe,

seamlessly merging   *in & out*

of one another   *mid suspension*
bridge over   *a bottomless*
canyon   *lifetime of grief*

it was a meeting of parallel nexuses
I was, he was, we were – sensitized proprioception

[Fg=Gm1m2r2]

beyond our   *years, bona fide*

scintillant   *greater than*

the sum

of our celestial parts

combined, we were

somehow—

our first night in VR was fleshlier than primal,
avatar to avatar – more human than human,

inside & out – in the vortex of a perfect storm,
our bodies one super cell,

our particles melded and our constellations
formed one new star,

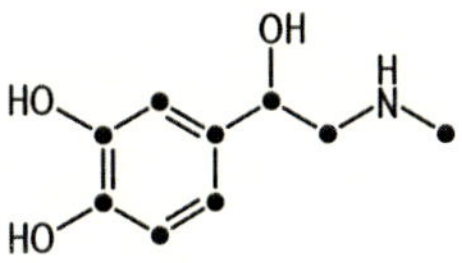

[ellipses perpetually bookended by unrounded
brackets].

Come to. Wait! Where am I? I don't know.
Oh yeah, on the couch, in sync.

Right. Oh yeah, bourbon. Bad idea.

Rain's Data Log

Private Notes XXVI – Veisalgia Incoming

Ow! Ow! Ow! What the...

Head throb, maelstrom strumming optic nerves.
Skull vice. Death grip of last night's debauchery.

Dry heave. Seasick. Woman overboard!

Crawling across a hangover wasteland, mouth
dry as sand. Sacré bleu, underwater blur, out
of focus. What was I thinking? Hocus pocus.

Snippets are coming back to me, snapshot. Oh no!
I was sloppy. When the DOD find out they'll come
and execute me. No! Gotta choose a new trajectory.
Copy that.

No, first they'll label me a political dissident, then
they'll concoct a bogus treasonous accusation.

I'll suffer some terrible accident like everyone
else. Another lowly dissident. An unfortunate
accident. An untimely demise.

The death certificate will read: fell down the stairs,
died of natural causes, accidental drowning, fatal
traffic accident, suicide, resisting arrest, et alii, killed
in a crossfire, a security operation gone amiss, snafu.

I've gotta stop this ridiculous fish, it's out of control.
There's only one answer and that is to withdraw
my Project O application and return the funding.
Affirmative.

Then it will all be over. I'll feign naivety, stupidity,

and I'll start taking the MetaNoia Pill again, yeah, I'll get a job and return to the repetitious slog.

Right, I'll bury the evidence, cover my tracks, leave zero footprint. They'll never know. *No. They'll know.*

Shite! Stand up. I'm literally reeling. Need a strong painkiller. *I can do it. Why am I standing?* I'm literally falling. *Am I standing?* Blur walking, turning, reeling. Don't think I can swallow a pill. *Just do it.*

Thirsty, but I can't drink. No! I have to H2O. Gag! Choke it back. Swallow. About to pass out. Where am I? Kitchen. I live here. Really, this is living? Oh, why is this happening?

What would Gauge do? Wait, did I call him last night? *I did. Right. Oh no. We talked.* Did I call him? No, he called me. *Did he?* He did. *I can't remember. Frig!*

Headlong, full-fledged vertigo.

Experiencing a veisalgia dizzy spell. Need to sleep this off. Crawl into the couch blankets ZZZZZZZZ

⁂

Holy crap. How long was I out? It's pitch black. Must've slept the entire day. Still have a headache. I'll keep the lights off. Where's my burner?

Feel my way around the apt's darkness by touch. It's easy to navigate ∵ everything's in place. Find waterglass on the kitchen. H2O. Sip as I cross back. Sit on couch drowning in confusion. Feel for burner. Find Dodecahedron. Hold it as a keystone.

The night light throws deep purple shadows around 303A. As I rub the Gad, it zaps me *ZZZZTTTT. Weird, electrical shocks from a polytope. What's it telling me?*

Jet: It's telling you to hold it for protection.

I blurt out, "Protection!" Why did I just say that?

Jet: Because I said it inside your head.

What? Who are you?

Jet: Jet.

Jet: Jet who?

Jet: Jet to you.

You?

Jet: Me. To you.

Are you trying to confuse me? Are you Ovoid? ΑΘΕ*'s friend?*

Jet: Yes, and I'm here to assist you. But we don't have much time.

What are you talking about?

Jet: What are YOU talking about?

How is this conversation even happening?

Jet: Telepathically.

It's impossible to perceive things that don't

exist. [n-sphere inside an n-spheres' n-sphere]

Jet: Could've fooled me. That aside, you need to focus. The Willows await your return. We're concerned about your safety.

The Willows?

Jet: The Shoal at Sweven. It's become more dangerous than we thought. I'm checking to see if you need help.

I'm a lowly insomniac scientist trying to decrypt this coded world, which is unravelling quickly and reality is travelling dérive and I'm an atomic minnow. On top of everything time is dissolving.

I can't lucidly fish yet, on my own I mean, I can't untie the Oneironaut of confusion. All my fishes seem to come from or belong to someone else and I can't sleep unless I'm tanked.

Jet: Maybe you should declare defeat and return to the life from which you came.

What?! No! I can't.

Jet: Then stop making excuses and dig deeper.

How? How do I do that?

Jet: Ask yourself why you want to fish.

Rhetorical?

Jet: No.

Why?

Jet: Why's often the question, in question.

I want to fish ∵ there's more to life than living dead. I can't swim and yet I keep ending up, landing in the deep end, swimming. Reptiles keep appearing and I'm not a snake person either!

Jet: Not! You may want to revisit the stories you've been telling yourself.

I've got more important concerns than navel gazing. Namely, do the DOD suspect me? Am I caught in the loop of a paradoxical net, an enigma?

Jet: May the east wind never blow.

Excuse me... ?

Jet: Stop leading with self determination. Surrender to your other self.

What does that look like? I'm more concrete than that!

Jet: Cement mixer mind will give you a wicked brain block. I'm talking about your higher self.

Higher? How do I do that?

Jet: You can't fish, or get a grip, so give up, abandon ship. But you still must return to Sweven ASAP.

If I abandon ship, I'll be a never-wazzer forever.

Jet: Listen! Intel tells us the DOD are onto you. You're putting your life in danger and the lives of all other fishers. Don't be so selfish!

What am I supposed to do... leave my life behind?

Jet: Look out your window. The DOD are in front of your building right now moving in to arrest you.

I peak through the slats in my blinds. She's right. Lucky I'm in the dark. They don't know I'm home.

Jet: Listen. The blue Ruin's parked three blocks north and around the corner. The keys are on top of the tire, drivers-side. Drive west, stick to the backroads. Look for new frontiers. Use an alias. Leave no digi-trail, or trackable devices. No plastic. Cash only. Do you have cash?

Uncle Ed always taught me to have mad money squirrelled away.

Jet: Then get it and go, now!

No time to think, I rip the envelop filled with loot off the back of the fridge. Hear the flipping ultracrepidarians bash down the lower front door.

Fast as a Spirostomum, I fly around #303A throwing things into my knapsack.

The Gad's fixed to the lifeline in my hand *SLIP SLIDE* zero vector enigma into my jacket pocket, could be a key, a watchword entity. Mad dash, grab hoodie, burner, glasses, and other sundry things.

Jet: Now climb out the window!

Notebook of LM

Entry XI – Facing Anathema

Think fast. Swing the fizgig at breakneck
speed.

Ouch! The key frostbites my hand, drop it,
crash. Sound of glass shattering amplifies
on the ceramic floor. Wound in a tight coil.

I jump out of my skin. Stress apex nerve chill,
pins and needles, inner freezer burn twinge,
edgy hypno-thermia, singe.

Advance across the barbed glacial minefield
to open the closet doors on the other side.

The Oneiroi resurrect in all their infernal glory,
and bash their black wings against the inside
the closet. They shoot flaming arrows at me
through the slats in the folding doors.

I've heard stories, that if a spark hits your skin
you're toast, but I'm not buying that anymore.

Fake it. Make like I'm a warrior and forge ahead.
I scream, you can't stop me this time! I possess
the power of the Fates! And in a Sailfish flash,
I open the demented closet doors in one svelte
movement! Anastasis!

A high-pitched shriek pierces my skull, the tone
splinters my thoughts, stiffens my endoskeleton.
My vision blurs me nauseated.

My affront enrages the Oneiroi. The attic thunders
and it explodes ecstatic super-nova. Sparks fly. A fire

breaks out all around me in dramatic arcs.
Can't tell what's real and what's not.

Skewed by fire and ice, I stop thinking and instinct
becomes my guide. I snap-shapeshift into my Merself
and scream a siren song.

My future-self makes decisions for my present
self from outside-itself in chronomantic spidey-
senses,

it manifests into a prismatic whirlwind ZZZZZ
ZZZZZ.

The williwaw turns the attic sky to outer space,
clusters of stars celestialize,

a galaxy of surreal eyes cry an atmospheric river,
Boreas and they extinguish the Oneiroi fire.

Everything stops.

<<<<<<<i will try to hold them back
until you find your wings>>>>>>>

Frozen in shock, drenched in irrational tears,
for the first time in years, I feel my old self
returning to me. Maybe it's a sign my O-naut
self will breathe and whisper in me again.

No idea what just happened. Breathe. Breathe.
My heart beats bat wings. I exhale stygian.

Listen and wait for a counterattack. Nothing
comes. Time loops into a hole, a loophole
hole,

my outside strife echo's my inside strife,
the hostile fight

constricts, it wraps itself around my neck,
it tightens its coils in a vicious circle – it swallows
me whole – alive – inside a kind of death.

The stench of evil is crushing!

I gather my nerve, look inside the closet,
face all the wonders I brought back from
my fishing expeditions with Che,

wonders of the whorl world, all rara avis.

Rain's Data Log
Private Notes XXVII – Make a Run For *IT!*

Never have I ever climbed out a window to escape.

So, what the hell am I doing? How can I be scaling along a narrow ledge on the outside of a window? *Is this me inching toward a getaway? Truly mortifying for an acrophobe.*

I slither along the side of the building, out of sight, mouse stuck to an adhesive surface. Change mind. I'm a wing walker, a precision paraglider. *What next?*

I'm an aerialist in a circus. *I can do this.* Can't.

SLAMBANG! The DOD SWAT team breaks down my door. Inner quail, really? They didn't even knock. *This is worse than I thought. A bust.* I'm being busted.

Can hear them crashing through my things, ransacking and they're hollering, but to no avail ∵ I wrote my notes in invisible ink. *Darknet!* Should've burned them. Overkill. *Is it?*

Dizzy with fear and vertigo, I scale the ledge, a suicide jumper, no, a circus act.

I close my eyes. A-b-o-u-t t-o d-i-e.

$$Zn+1 = Zn^2 + C$$

FAR FLUNG MADNESS

PING! Where am I?

Standing on the edge of a bluff, overlooking the sea, pungent tang of salt & fish, decaying seaweed,

I'm filled with a sensation unfamiliar to me, simultaneously paradisiacal and maniacal.

<<<<<<<jump>>>>>>>

What? No!

<<<<<<<just jump>>>>>>>

No! I can't. I'll kill myself.

Something shoves me from behind. I fly over the cliff,

"Aaaahhh."

I splash into the sea, *not again, how many times do I have to tell you, fish,* "I can't friggin' swim."

(δ θ γ dream end)

I land standing on the sidewalk right below my apartment building,

soaking wet & it's not raining, *hahaha—*

What just happened... ?

Jet: Run. Run! RUN!

I can't. I can't move. I'm paralysed.

Jet: Unstick yourself. You must make a run for it. NOW!

I'm deactivated, *I can't friggin' move.*

Jet: Run for your Ruin. You must do this for us all.

I can't, I'm drowning in hodophobia, existential angst, I'm having a catatonic episode, a face-off with myself.

Jet: You'll die if you stay in this mindset. Sorry, something's jamming us. Have to dematerialize before I'm detected...

What...? Hello Jet?! Where are you? Dang! She's gone.

When did my *to do* list turn into my *to don't do* list? *Don't do it.* Tick. *Don't do it.* Tick. *Don't.*

Above me, the DOD police bark out orders at one another. Their rabid sounds defenestrate like large combustible appliances.

Every cell in my body explodes with cytolysis?¿ ?¿ Darknet! Must escape X-City before they catch me. *No, it's too dangerous.*

I'm torn ∵ I know leaving is for good. *So why can't I?* If I run and then they catch me it will be way worse. *It's too late.* Not! Don't do it. *Don't not do it.* Just go!

I'm experiencing post-MetaNoia paranoia. PTSD from a lifetime of tyranny. *Just do it. Don't not do it. Just do it.* Don't. *So panicked I think I just peed a bit.*

Internal power struggle. *My mind's fighting the grip fear it has on itself*, pulling in the opposite direction.

What if I never see Gauge or my mother again?
I'm fighting myself fighting myself, meta-meta-clash.
I must unstick myself.

I shift fraction-by-fraction until my feet are free and I flee toward Ruin. Act normal. Run, but don't run! No sudden movements, hoodie up to help me disappear. I hear a black bird screech – after dark, peculiar, almost jump out of my skin.

$Zn+1 = Zn^2 + C$

Cognitive dissonance. Fear shoots out of my eye sockets. I can't breathe.

Omnidirectional scan for curfew police. Only see shadows and sharp corners, streetlights glare down – become interrogation beams, but they make the glasphalt twinkle with little road stars. The presence of the unseen looms & lurks. Eyes watch everywherein the darkness They mask their hungry fangs behind the eerie silence.

Out of my wits, my brain beats from my temples. Dizzy stareyes – turbo adrenaline surges. My feet pound the pavement.

DEEPREM

SIMULTANEITY FUGUE

Sucked into the black Pearl Ovoid of tenebrosity, devoid of light, blank slate. *Thank you, Jet!*

Is this a fish? Reality check. Am I or am I not,

fishing? Look down at my hand, yes, there's no Merrow.

A hypnotic voice echoes in the distance along biosonic sound waves – follow me))) me)))) me))))) and hurry)))))) quickly))))))).

Parallel plane: Run lickety-split between the shafts in the shadows of streetlights. Flip—

Standing in the onyx black Ovoid barefoot. Coolness stings the soles of my feet, cobblestones, maybe iridescent labradorite. *[(Ca, Na)(Al, Si)4O8]*

Not a trace of light, running through pre-creation darkness, the blade of an obsidian knife. Running blindfolded toward a sonic boomerang.

Parallel pinball: Dodge X-City street cams, wizard mode. A multiball rampage, DO NOT TILT! Haha. Flip—

Whose fish is this anyway? Is oneirokinesis a thing? Am I experiencing dream telepathy from another ~~dream~~ fish transferee. *[E=hv]*

Weird! Can't tell if my eyes are open or closed, but somehow, I know I'm Hygieia. *Am I?*

Parallel frame: Run for my life! Pounding boots behind me, echo off the streets, then resound off buildings, as they close in tighter, almost ready to bite my heels. Three blocks feel transcontinental. Flip—

[TrEs-2b]
The mesmeric voice hisses, follow)))))))))))))))

))) the sonic trail)))) of my voice)))))) faster))))))).

Absorption, distortion, into a hypnotic trance.
If I were a tenrec, I'd tap my quills for echolocation,
but I'm not, so I don't. The darkness shifts me
past fear. It shifts me into non-existence.
At this point I'm on autopilot.

***Parallel reality: Overexertion short windedness,
wheezy, seeing stars. Spot blue Ruin, trice skewered
by the sharp spit of hope. Retrieve the key, slink
along the side, slide inside, flushed in neurogenic
shock.***

***In the black Pearl, Hun state of the Tardigrade,
check out the backseat. Gauge is there, lying
face-up, holding the hubcap to his chest. Flip—***

Hygieia is becoming nyctophiliac inside the cave
of the Delphic Bee. Some people function better
in the dark – they never turn the lights on.

Woozy & disoriented, impossible to find a shadow
in an ebon quantum state. Pythia ghosts in & out
of my vision. She wavers hinkypunky. Here, then,
not there. There, then, not here.

***Parallel flight: Ruin starts! Gauge is fast asleep.
"Gauge wake up! Wake up!" Ruin purrs, her purr
echoes off the buildings held captive in the silence
of the curfew. I yell over my shoulder, "Come on.
Wake the fuck up, Gauge!" At the same time, I roll
out, quiet as a mouse meme, with headlights off.
Can no longer determine what's a fish and what's
nought. Flip—***

In & out of flickering light, in the flash of a single strobe, I catch a snap-glimpse of the Oracle Pythia in silhouette. She's perched high on a gold tripod.

In the in & out of the light pulse I time warp, not unlike glimpsing into a glitch, I see the unticking chronostasis of lost eternities. *Really?* Really.

And within the hiccup I epiphanize that as Hygieia, Pythia & I know each other very well. *Cool! In & out. In & out. In & out.*

Parallel path: Moans from the backseat. I drive blue Ruin down the secret side streets of X-City, at hyperspeed. Escape. Escape. Double padiddle, hairpin corner on two wheels, no key to this riddle.

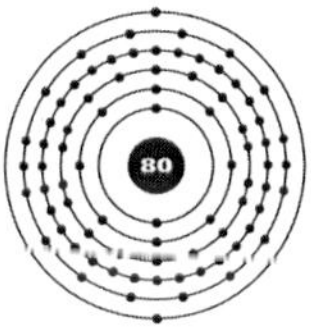

Driving so fast the streetlights zoetrope. Smell of burning rubber. How did Gauge end up here? Flip—

Sink to the feldspar floor at the feet of the Oracle Pythia, the great diviner.

In & out, she closes her fantascopic eyes, presses her lips to the air – to the sky, she feigns a long kiss as if shared with an illusory lover – perhaps it's the gesture of good-bye or then again, maybe it's the sweet mirage of hello, after many years apart.

I trace the outline of her breast nipples, erect through her see-through mid-night blue chiton.

Inhalation of ecstasy, I breathe hallucinogenic vapors as they rise from the rock below me. Her body coils sensorial, tingles me wild. Beguiled, I fall under her museful, no, her mazeful spell.

I'm struck with seeing into her traumatic past, which has become intertwisted with mine. *Are we forever responsible for the actions of parents? Forebearers?*

Here I am, Hygieia – at the hands of my new-found father, Apollo.

The vision comes to me in a split-second Nova—

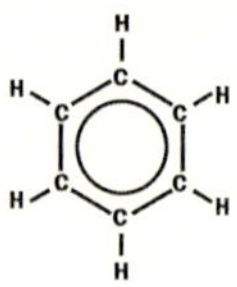

my father, Apollo, draws back his bow & aims
the rancor of old family revenge at the Python,
sometimes retrocognition is worse than prophesy.

He releases one-hundred arrows at once. He slays the Python. The Python was sent by Gaia [the earth] to safe-guard the Oracle of Delphi,

& as the Python dies,
as she lets go of her soul
I can see her soul, as it lets go
the mist & the vapor grows, I see

the flickering Python figure
with an ethereal glow,
as she enters the body of the Oracle, I see
the Oracle accept the miraculous spirit
of the Python

into her living body,
I see the Oracle become Pythia
so, the Python might live inside her every breath
to live inside her every breath and sight
between reality & illusion
between the shadow

& ephemeral delusion
for all time in interstice
the holding bay of death & life

vapor rises

between the first breath & the last
we whirl
in & out of light
unnerved
unable to turn
back
wheels of wheels within wheels & wheels
of time

sleight of
hands of
kismet
of nemesis
of hubris
action
rolling into reaction
unfolding
the consequence of which
is knowing

nothing

time is more powerful than I.

Smells sweet in here. Breathe deep the gathering
ethylene, *is this me speaking? What susurrus is this?*

*What strange alchemy is this? What gives? Was that me
speaking, in transmigration?¿ ?¿ ?¿*

Is this the result of fish & reality bleeding together
into one causation.

Hypnotic, the Oracle Pythia turns & looks into me. With sibilant speech she "*HISSSes*, transfiguration. Yes, you have seen into the past & the sacred vapours have shown you the path. The lightning bolt of bliss has struck your death knell so you might reach into your full potential."

I immediately slingshot out of the stone abyss & into a neo-nether blackness, where I sense Pythia behind me breathing. She is the darkness itself. *[D001921] JUMP.*

Parallel empuzzlement: I am, what I am not. And I am not, where I think I am. I am whizzing around the last roundabout before the final stretch out of X-City. No lights. Hoping the magic happens before the trick hits, navigating a road I've only taken once before – maniac heretic, in the dark. Flip—

Being pulled down, drowning in a pool of Castalian waters, gasp, just inhaled the whole spring, grasping for a non-existent rope, flapping, gasping, yelping, "Help! Help!"

My cries are lost to a loud sea.

The water is over my head – thrown into the deep end of death. Vanishing beneath the surface of my own unreal breath, I yell out, "I called this world onto myself."

Pounding at the temple door, I gasp, hard core gasping for air, screaming, "I can't swim. Let me in. Let me in!"

Pythia's voice rings through the frightmare, "Remember who you are & also who you aren't. You're inside the Temple of Dreams – where the only

limitations that exist are the ones that you enlist
in your own mind."

"I heard that Pearl before. Bought the bumper
sticker, sold the car. It's hard to drive when you
know you're drowning."

Pythia hisses, "Then stop drowning and swim."

Right, delirium dells as I quell my capsized mind,
"Is this my story or someone else's game?"

Asp, "They're one in the same – you are, they are,
we are, one. You must survive to End Game, Rain,
to save the Serpent Dragon, the Secret Order of Nauts
& all reverie."

Alpha out. She vanishes. Poof, into an invisible
axion & I'm left all alone without a fish in the world.

Parallel perplexity: A hoarse voice from the back-
seat seeks, "where the fuck am I?" No time to reply.
Must drive the night umbral with all my might.
I drive with all synapses firing. Lucky I'm neuro-
divergent. My superpower is definitely a laser focus.

(δ θ γ dream end)

Notebook of LM
Entry XII – Whispers of the Dead

Rara avis piscis. Wonder what wonder is.
Rummage through the closet of no-return.

<<<<<<<don't dillydally, Lily>>>>>>>

Old coats hang beside forgotten realms,
their memories cast long shadows.

Doubloons from a shipwreck, treasures
gather dust. Comb through cast-off get-ups
and magical artifacts, vials of corked fish.
Lichen! Not certain what I'm looking for.

Plundering the past churns up antiquated
emotions, scrapes them raw again, trauma
tears fly. Remember sunken cities.

I lift my emotional blindfold, blink, my eyes
sensitive to sight, blink, blink, mixed emotions
sandwiched between nostalgia and regret.

Newsflash to self. I'm exposing my enduring
soul in some kind of anamorphosis.

<<<<<<<you're light on time, Lily,
stay focused>>>>>>>>>>>>>>

O Barnacles! I don't know what I'm looking for,
but I remember this basket of extinct seashells
that Che and I collected on a jump out-of-time.

Nuance sifts through closet wreckage and lifts
a pocket watch up by its chain in his beak.

And this timepiece with ancient bells and chimes,
we were keeping to exchange for another parrot.

SQUAWK! With his wings in a flap, he scolds me.
What? You brought me back from a fish? *OH NO!*
Is that how you got me? Is this my origin story?
OH NO! Are you telling me I'm a fish bird?

Sorry, Nuance, Sorry. We don't have time for this
right now. I'll tell you the story later!

<<<<<<<stay focused>>>>>>>

SHRIEK! Did you hear that? His feathers are seriously
ruffled – in a flurry.

I try to reassure him. No, I didn't. Don't scare me.
We need to stay focused.

HOOTHOOT! Am I hearing in double?

No, but you're speaking in it!

SQUAWK! That's not what I meant. Forget it!
The past is prologue. It's prologue! You got this.

Quondam and perpetuity are era-blending.
Don't know why we kept this useless stuff,
dried flowers, porcupine quills, a driftwood
walking stick.

*<<<<<<<enchanted curios is why – time's scarce
move faster>>>>>>>*

CLICKCLICK! Did you hear that? Just now!
It sounded like Che.

What are you taking about, Nuance?

CLICKCLICK! From dream room to death tomb.
Che. Not everyone can master grief. *SQUAWK!*

Now he's ruffling my feathers, as I continue
digging through odds and ends, I say to him,
once you know the combination to the safe,
your life's always in danger.

HOOTHOOT! What are you talking about?
And what's this? A bird's nest. Oh no. Oh no!
You brought someone's home back with you.
The air looms with doom!

Sorry, dear. We'll talk later. I'm having trouble
seeing with all this noise. Need silence in order
to look into things and see.

TRILLTRILL! Love it when you shush me.
Shush me!

Look at these, Nukey, I forgot about these blue
ribbons shaped into butterflies, and this, this
ship lost in a bottle.

SHRIEK! EEK! That's what happened to Atlantis.
I've seen them all. All sinking, sinking in beauty,
beauty sinking. Ys, Lyonesse, Lumeria, et cetera,
et cetera, cetera. They all sank in a lost bottle!
FLIBBERTY-FLUE!

Funny you. And I've spent too many moons
drawing elusive Runes, waiting for the naut
of reverie to return to me.

SQUAWK! Empty vessel makes the loudest

sound. Melancholia will destroy ya. Blue. Make you blue, in the face, mask of death, death, death, don't take your last breath.

Nuance flies in circles around the attic, leaves a contrail of color behind him. I cry out, when dreams are taken from us, we stop imagining what we might have been, we start accepting what is.

CLICKCLICK! This is not a drill. You can't see what you believe doesn't exist.

I'm tired of swimming in circles until I wear a trench in the water.

Nuance flies into the closet, lands on top of the hangers. *HOOTHOOT!* Cowards die many times, before their demise.

Paraphraser!

SQUAWK! Be brave.

<<<<<<<hurry up, Lily>>>>>>>

SQUAWK! Did you hear that? Hear that?

What?

<<<<<<<find the wings>>>>>>>

SQUAWK! That. That voice! Did you hear it? Hear it?

What voice?

The voice that said, look for wings. The wings.
The voice said look for wings. Hurry scurry flurry.
Wings. Wings! *WINGS!*

No, I didn't hear a voice, but *PLING. TWANG.* Look
at this. My insight wings. I forgot about these things.
Wonder if they'll work for an X-O-naut stripped
of her fishes. Can you feel the saudade, Nukey?

*<<<<<<<take them for a spin around sky
Empyrean>>>>>>>*

Che and I would fly with these wings for hours,
and they'd help us think laterally, they'd broaden
our attitudes with soaring altitudes, the big picture.

*<<<<<<<oh no – you're about to be ambushed by
Oneiroi Daemons>>>>>>>*

Sky-Fly-Fishing. We etched silken lines across
the lapis lazuline expanse.

Sinister sounds erupt from the quarry of the closet.

SQUAWK! Grab your wings and let's scram, Lily,
let's get out of here, now!

Rain's Data Log

Private Notes XXVIII – Blue Streak of Genius

Jump into parallel world – the origin dimension
aka reality – and I'm driving. Wonder how long
I've been driving without knowing I'm driving.

Gauge is regaining consciousness in the backseat.
"Rain, what's happening!?"

I over-the-shoulder remark, "I'll explain everything
when the system's stable."

SOS! SOS! Jet! Jet! Jet!

*Jet: I can only hold you in invisibility mode 'til you reach
X-City limits. Once you're outside The Grille, you two
are on your own.*

That would've been nice to know in advance!

Almost at the limits! *That's the first time I've heard
X-City called The Grille. Perfecto!*

On the move, Ruin blue, incognito. *Old skool cars
are mostly black, white, or grey. Ergo if I wasn't invisible,
I'd stick out like an audacious accusation,*

*an envy-fuelled bald-faced lie concocted to cancel a peer
you're competitive with. To deceive hordes of gullible,
yet useful idiots into hate clicking. Where did that come from?*

It's not leaving X-City that scares me, it's returning
to no one and nothing, nostophobia. Rear view mirror,
clear, not being tailed by the shadow. Gauge says,
"Hello! Calling Rain from the backseat."

I reply, "Still driving in hyper-warp speed to escape the DOD. Sorry, all eyes on drive."

The Bureau's made us all oneirophobic—*TURNLEFT*—politicophobic—*LEFT*—and we believed them—*RIGHT*—took the pill—*TURNRIGHT*—abjectly—*LEFT*—I worked for them.

I actually left #303A. Now, a perfect stranger will move in and fill in the gap of me, in a sense they'll be the turnkey me. And the new me will likely live my life better than I did.

No one behind me yet. Guess Jet's cloak is working.

Eventually, the new me will grow sick of their tedious life, and they'll move their life to a new location. No! Even if I do return, my life's officially over. It will not be where I left it. Darknet!

What if No. 303A decides it hates itself and determines to throw the contents of itself out the window onto the sidewalk below.

Effigy of a scarecrow. Drive into the wilderness of not-knowing. Didn't know the wilderness still existed outside of VR, but it does.

ROUNDABOUTTURN—didn't notice the iron fist behind the lotus flower of false promises—*EXIT RIGHT*—boiling frog apologue of maleficent smiles—*SHARPTURN*—they're eccedentesiasts—fake as a foe's handshake—all grip, no guts—*TURNLEFT*—ribbit.

The opposite of AI is definitely HS (human stupidity).

No. There's no coming back from where I'm headed, we're headed. How did Gauge get here anyway?

There it is. The X-City city limits sign,

topographagnosiated,

slow,
gear down,
down,
down,

disorientated,

once we cross the line,
we've really crossed the line,

about to leave invisibility,
behind,

not phenomenology,

a threshold, an imaginary line
of the outer periphery,

aka Ephialtes,

3-2-1-zero.

Cross over,
a kind of death,

obit of no-return.

"Fasten your seat belt Gauge,
we'll never unlearn
what we're about to know,
or, where we're about to go.

Throw all devices out the window."

"None followed me, except this random hubcap."

"We're officially free!"

He decrees, "—or we're officially screwed."

Notebook of LM

Entry XIII – Phantom Reappearance

SNAP! The trapdoor shuts. *CLICK!* The hatch
latch locks. Scramble down the bean stalk.

Nuance screams wildly beside me, *SQUAWK!*
Everything's higgledy-piggledy, Lily. Piggledy-
higgledy. Topsy-turvy. Upside-down. *WHAW!*

Reach ground level. Dogs bark hysterically,
terror-stricken, cats clawing, Geckos squalling
deranged, Orangutan. Try to find centre.

Slide the key into my pocket. The hands on all
the clocks are spinning backwards, gyroscopic, the hall
mirror coruscates in a flash, it turns black,

electricity shoots through every wire of The Clove,
as if we just took a direct hit, struck by multi-forked
prongs of lightning – retribution in the form of instant jinx.

Nuance *TRILLS.* Hijinks. Hijinks!

Psychic parrot. I etch an apotropaic hexafoil, sigil
of protection into the air, sky engraving. Sparks
fly from my fingertips.

Shumba barks in distressed claxons, as does Violet.
Their tails twirl in terror. Together, they question
me with widened eyes, I can see it. What kind
of purgatory is this?

Their expressions tell me it's time to communicate.
Holding the wings, I step into position for spiritual
tribunal.

Standing on three points, our triad triangulates in the centre of the sunroom. The others gather around.

We begin rapid-eye contact, an askance glance dance, signalling inner truths to one another, the meaning, subtext and essence which cannot be conveyed, only transmitted and approximated.

Me to Shumba—sorry my friends, it was time I faced the problem head-on.

Shumba to Violet—we must support Lily.

Violet to me—you are risking our lives.

Me back to Violet—I am sorry, I couldn't live with Oneiroi hanging over our heads any longer. I must find out the truth about Che.

Violet to Shumba—she's right, we're all in this together.

Shumba to all—we are one another. The beast council declares this,

ᛊᚨᚲᚱᛖᛞ ᚨᛊᛊᛖᛗᛒᛚᛁ
ᚹᛁᛚᛚ ᚢᛈᚱᛁᛊᛖ ᛁᚾ ᚦᛖ ᚾᚨᛗᛖ ᛟᚠ ᚺᚨᚱᛗᛟᚾᛁ

Despite the resolve, in the dwindling aftermath, our glances advance with foreboding, knowing by addressing the unmentionable, we agree to make huge changes in our lives.

Given they're egolessness, lingo-coding's faster in beasts than in humans.

Next the council disbands quicker than I'm able
to integrate.

I interrupt—I retrieved these wings to advance
the process of healing, my O-naut, and otherwise.

They respond from various points of departure
and a menagerie of sound fills the sunroom.

I say, tomorrow, Nukey and I will fly at dawn.
This spawns a cacophony of yeses, which infuses
the air with jubilation. I am blessed.

Rain's Data Log
Private Notes XXIX – Past Bleeds into Present

"Where in tarnation are we?" from the backseat.

I want to say, we just jumped from a simple prokaryote to a complex eukaryote cell, but I don't. Last time this was a lot less meaningful. Instead, I answer, "We just left X-City limits. *SNAP!* We're on the other side of the great divide. We crossed over the invisible line that's been holding us prisoner."

Gauge answers, "O... kay... "

"Can't talk right now. Gotta drive like stink. Need you to keep your eyes peeled for the DOD."

"Okay... "

I'm reseized by a wicked I'd-rather-die than persist-to-exist hangover. Dang! I was so distracted I didn't even notice it for the last chaotic hour or so, but now it's back with a full-frontal brain-throb vengeance! I ask Gauge, "You don't happen to have a painkiller, do you?"

A murmur rises from the backseat, "Are you kidding me right now?"

"Sorry, no, I'm sorry. Everything's just haywire."

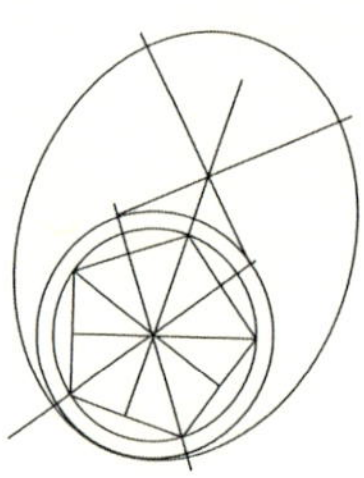

∵ ∴ *Observation Deck* ∴ ∵
Endosymbiosis – is a symbiotic relationship where one organism lives inside another.

He asks, "Are you alright?"

"My bean's been beheaded and my noggin's being served up on a platter, sans a body. It's a big cluster-fluck. Feel like I'm cracking up."

"Right. You called me last night. Better to swipe left," he says.

"I called you? Right, I did speak to you. But it was you who called me?"

"Oh yeah, it was me."

Drive on MacWheezy, drive on. I make light of the situation, "I'm so crossic right now, I'm hanging onto the grass to stop myself from flying right off the planet earth."

He smirks, "Last night you said, 'I'm drinking from the bottle of a merciless ghost,' you said, 'There is no glory, where there is no mirth.'"

"I don't know why I said that."

"I've never known you drink like that."

Darknet! "Well, I—"

Jet: I only have a moment. You're unmaskable.

Where am I going?

Jet: Can't reveal that. Just drive.

What about the Ovoid for transport, the black Pearl?

Jet: Can't run the risk of exposing you to Ovoid-bends, which we don't fully understand... but we do know overuse is too dangerous.

"Ovoid-bends?"

Jet: Sorry, I've been detected. Going dark.

Gauge asserts, "Are you alright?

"No. Yes. Just distracted is all."

Wish I could morph myself into sublimation,
isomerization, absolute transmutation.

Still feel Hygieia in my bones, lucid as a far off echo, but I still can't fish on demand. Weird, my last fish's coming back to me,

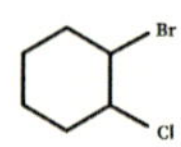

Pythia
said
something
like

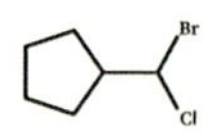

'... survive to End Game, save the Serpent Dragon, the Secret Order of Nauts, something something, reverie.' *Holy cray-cray fish!*

∵ ∴ Mental Note ∴ ∵
If there's a way to jog a fish memory, there must be a way to go back and retrieve it.

Back there, as we hit the city sign, I looked down. There was a Merrow!

I am.
I am nought,
in a fish.

From the backseat, Gauge leans in close enough that I can feel his breath as he speaks, "I hate to be a backseat driver, but where are we going, Rain?"

"I can't tell you ∵ if I tell you I'll have to kill you.
I don't know. I really can't explain anything ∵
it's unexplainable, like a UFO visitation."

"Okay."

"Why don't you climb into the front seat?" Gauge,
an ardent geek who's never been particularly agile
dives over the seat headfirst which is hilarious
and despite our precarious situation, within seconds
we're both howling so hard I almost run off the road.

When the dust settles, Gauge probes in singsong,
"What's going on?"

"So much, I don't know where to begin. I don't know
how you got here, but I'm glad you're here."

"Well, I'll tell you. One minute I was at my station
and the next I was in the backseat hugging a hubcap."

"Okay Gauge, shorthand. First, I stopped taking
the MetaNoia."

He goes, "Copy." Then, "I found the Oneironaut article
and went on that trip to Sweven."

He goes, "Right... "

"And then I got back and the DOD have been tailing
me ever since. Somehow... "

"Wait. I've got something to tell you first... " He says,
"I stopped taking the pill too... just after you got back."

"Really! Have you fished yet?"

"Might have. Can't be too sure."

"Has anyone spoken to you? Inside your head?"

He goes, "No, but I did end up in your backseat."

"Right, and now we're trying to outrun the DOD, so, I guess you're coming with me."

"It's about time we did a real-life adventure together. Where are we headed?"

"I think... back to Sweven... with the help of Jet."

"Propulsion?"

"No. I'll tell you about her later. And for your information, I'm lucid as a glacial lake."

"Should I congratulate you?"

"You can if you want! I've gone googolgon, turned infinitesimally infinitesimal." *[CH4+C2H6+C3H8+C4H10]*

"Are you okay? Do you want me to drive?"

"Yes, no, I got this."

THE BUREAU
DEPARTMENT OF DREAMS
SECURITY INTELLIGENCE REPORT
CODE RED—MOST WANTED

File: 210178MS5F
Date/Time: Future Continuous Tense
Subject: Rain (ID # 220 455 816)

ESCALATED VIOLATION REPORT:
Escaped Arrest.
Escaped Parameter.

Verified Association w/ Dissidents.
Nox Chieftain Dreamer – Probable Mutated Oneironaut.

Believed Armed & Dangerous.

OFFICIAL STATUS:
Threat Advisory.
Believed to be Driving Automobile.
(Rent-a-Ruin)

RECOMMENDATION:
Apprehend Alive.

Panopticon Surveillance # 220 002 336 – Perp's Mother.

________________*below the bottom line*________________

Office of Dr. Lester Maggott, inside The Bureau.

Shelly grovels, then replies in a shrill obedient voice, "Yes sir, experiencing some interference is all, sir."

"Shelly, are you listening?"

Out of breath, Shelly squeaks, "Yes sir, yes sir, I'm listening, listening, but... "

Maggott snaps his fingers in her face, "I want your full undivided attention. Don't want you to screw this one up!"

Shelly kowtows between shutters and stutters, glassing over, "I'm l-l-listening, sir." She fidgets with her jumpsuit zipper.

Maggott's voice rumbles with a heavy bass tone, "I want you to expedite a global WW all points BOLO, immediately, Shelly!

Citizen # 220 455 816 is a fringe dissident, enemy of the state, to be found, captured and brought to justice by sundown.

Mark my words, this Rain is either a Nox Chieftain, or some kind of mutationally advanced O-naut, the likes of which we haven't seen since NC1SU.

Listen up! I smell the noxious stench of insurgency upon us and it's closing in – tighter than a skull-crushing vice device."

"Ouch! The cost would be worth our lives, sir."

"Our mole tells us there's a revolt brewing inside a fringe rebellion somewhere on the outside. Intel says, there's a group of dreamers plotting a coup."

"Oh no, no, no!" Shelly, self-flagellates in advance.

"Yes. That's why we're in a state of emergency. Must act fast. Don't get the jitters Shelly, I want a full profile of # 220 455 816 on my desk by noon."

"Got it. Got it, sir! I thought you said sundown."

"Are you listening? I just said... noon!"

Her boots obviously new, slide on the silk carpet and she literally spins several times before taking her leave.

Vexed watching her, Maggott snarls, "This time no excuses Shelly, no miscalculations!"

"Got it, sir. Don't forget your hard-hat for the... funding incentive photo-op you have in ten."

Notebook of LM

Entry XIV – Old Wings / New Feathers

Morning doesn't come fast enough. At the first glint of dawn, I'm out the door faster than gonzo beans en route to their first psychedelic party.

I whistle for Nuance to join me with our signature transcendental hoot – followed by, are you ready to rumble, Cha-Cha?

WHOOSH, Nuance flies in beside me, also kookily whistling, hooting. I love the way his wings bring life to the air. He lands on my shoulder.

I nudge the ridge of his abalone beak with my cheek and murmur to him, once upon a time we travelled to far off-world realms and returned with magical animisms, like these shape-shifting wings.

SHRIEK! I know, let's split this Lily pad.

Sshhh, keep your voice down, honey, we don't want to wake the mayhem of Geckoes.

Note: We whisper in the morning, so we don't startle the drift of our fishful thoughts.

Nukey nods, then cranes, to maximize my affections. I ruffle his head feathers with the tops of my fingertips, to receive ethereal sensations and I whisper, these wings aren't a mere souvenir, Nukey, maybe they'll fly me back to my old life.

SHRIEK! Old life! Old life! Che! Che! Che!

Shush, I say, still unable to face the loss of Che.

SHRIEK! Did you just shush me? *TSK! TSK! TSK!*

I did. But only to stop you from oversharing.

EEK! Never! Private! I'm a private parrot!

Bird on shoulder, wings in hand, I make my way
toward the littoral land.

Shadows shift to make room for light, dappling.

Nuance nuzzles me, singsongs loss, so much loss,
sometimes he's my therapist, sometimes my confidant.

As we traverse the path through the rainforest
I tell him a story, as I always do in the trees. I say,
these wings remind me of a shell we once brought
back from the sea with me and Che, yes,

she was gloriously unusual, out of the ordinary,
an extraordinarily superlative Queen Conch Shell,
found well below scuba depths.

TRILL! Deeper than the deepest abyssal depths!

I found her on the beach waiting for me, and I could
hear the entire sea of her when I pressed her inner lip
to my outer ear,

I can still see Che's eyes looking at me.

They say, you can't hear the sea, that it's not
really the sea that you hear,

but I could hear her seasong sing from the depths,
I could hear her surge and the undertow of her being,

of her waves as they tide-crossed the threshold of reality
and lapped against my vitality with the pulse of a pearl,

I could not leave her there on the far off beach
and I carried her sacred geometry back with me,

aperture to my ear to hear
her one, two : one, two.

TRILLTRILL! And silent three!

And I placed her on our windowsill –
and then one day I picked her up and listened
and I realized she herself was returning to the sea
esprit. As I held her to my ear and I knew it was
really her story to tell – of her loss.

YES!

The depth of her longing to be free wavered
in and out of me. I was besieged with regret
for removing her from the sands and the depths
of her being, luna moon current.

As I listened, I realized that's why she cries
deep song duende, in waves of sorrow,

she cries her story for all she has lost
and left behind.

SQUAWK! I marvel how fishes live in the sea...

Pericles! I choose not to answer that riddle.

TRILL! Thought I'd snare you with that one.

Not today, little Forever. Today I'm free
from trickery! And right then—

We arrive at the clearing. I place the wings
among the blossoms on the fringe of the wild-
flower field,

shadows open and sunrays break through
the cedars in ecotones,

a single beam of light lands on the sequestered
wings, astonishing.

Nuance riffs, beautiful wings, beautiful
golden wings!

I wonder if these beauties will remember
me and respond, I say.

SHRIEK! Encore, encore! How could they not!
How could they forget flying in a fish, and all things
left behind!

Rain's Data Log

Private Notes XXX – Spearheading Consciousness

I've officially arrived in the middle of nowhere, far outside the gates of The Grille, in the danger danger zone – the heart of forbidden wilderness with my BFF, Gauge, beside me.

Feel like we've been driving for eon-zoids.

Gauge attempts to amuse me with a surface-level deep dive, "The Golden Ratio appears throughout the natural world, in seen and unseen dimensions. But the pièce de resistance comes when you extend the lines of the sides of the 3-D pentagon – to get a pyramid, starlike cosmic harmony, ɸ symmetry."

"Indeed! But it seems like, if you strive for beauty, to make beauty, create it, there's always a non-fisher who thinks it's their duty to smash that beauty, yes, to trash that beauty and then crush you ∵ they want you to be closer to the room where they hang their nothing hat."

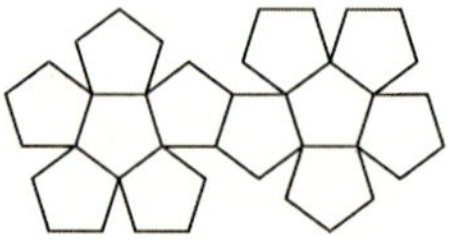

"Time for that to change!"

Death noodles! Hate to rain on our ratio parade, but there're headlights coming up behind us."

"Can't be," he says, "We've been driving for super-eons without seeing a single vehicle."

"I know, it's been a zero-traffic wasteland. So, where'd they come from in the darkness?" I ask.

"Likely the last on-ramp. Damn those friggin' feeder roads!"

"More like feeding frenzy roads! Shite!"

"Stay cool, stay positive, Rain."

"Nope. Yep, the car at our six o'clock is definitely tailing us with shark energy. They're probably a DOD SWAT Team."

He says, "Or the not-so-secret secret police."

"How did they track us? Worse, what if they catch us? We had a quantum scale head start."

"Just steer, no, veer away from your fear to avoid cranial apocalypse."

"Maybe they're analogous. Is that a word? *ZZIT–ZZIT!* My motherboard's short circuiting. I'm wigging out, maybe I'm coming to. Either way, if they catch us, we're royally screwed."

He goes, "Where's your friend, Jet?!"

"They're flashing their brights, zeroing in on us, for real. We're all alone in a no-go zone."

"You're not alone. We're in this together."

"Need more juice! Come on little blue Ruin rocket, give me all you got!"

"Pedal to the mental, Rain. You got this!"

"No advance enhance turbo." *Damn the DOD, for forbidding fishing ∵ fishing takes us to new levels of powerful, it takes us to a place where we see things we've never seen before.*

Gauge interjects, "My Kairotic take away... prepare to die... even if you plan not to!"

"Uncle Ed always said, 'Nothing makes a fish seem larger than almost getting caught.'"

"They're playing the equidistant game."

"We're being tied in a knot."

<<<<<<<fishing's your superpower>>>>>>>

What?! Next, you'll be telling me I'm a polar bear
who just gave birth to twins WHOOSHWHOOSH
easy as that - end of extinction.

Sounding slightly agitated, a first for Gauge, "Paradigm pivot. Slow down, test their patience, see if they pass."

<<<<<<<you're an uber-angler>>>>>>>

"Right!? Too many voices at once," I say.

Gauge replies, "Are you okay? Make space for them to pass, test the limits of their phishing expedition."

"Okay. Gearing down."

Where's my Dodecahedron?

Notebook of LM

Entry XV – Just Because You Have Wings…

This is not a simulation.

Close my eyes, envision the wings attaching
themselves to my bronzed shoulder blades,
as they once did in my time-out-of-time mind
immemorial.

I can't assume fish see as I see, or live as I live.
Must let go of all perceptions, give way to new
reflections, look through the eyes of a new fish
gaze. Try to see luminally again, everywhen
again, breathe,

the morning air senses the wings, caresses them,
feathers flutter in the zephyr, ever so slightly,
still slumberous after a long hibernation,

the wind takes her time, preens the wings serene,
reacquaints herself with her old friend – plume
after plume, plume,

the wings quiver, their ethereal dust whorls
up without skipping a tone, heartstrings sweep
into a long strum, the wings lift off the ground.
My eyes open to deep time,

the pinions attach themselves to my back,
irreversible and intangible – this is not a thought
experiment – their airfoil-age is undeniable.

I ascend into the crisp sunrise, Nuance
beside me. Widdershins, I curse, I'm awfully
wobbly!

SQUAWK! You are scrambled in chaos. Chaos!
You are out-of-order order!

Not! I can do this, Nuance!

SQUAWK! Parrots can fish with the best of 'em! *TRILL!*
You've got defective aerodynamics!

I check the back of my hand for the Ouroboros.
It's there. Which tells me I'm not fishing. I'm not.

SQUAWK! See! According to epochal news, news,
there was a time – time, when Mermaids flew, before
they turned exclusively to the sea, to the sea, sea.
Follow me, with your mind—

In my mind's-eye the blue of the sky is the blue
of the sea – as we rise up and up, the air tickles,
scales, skin and fin in a full body piloerection.

Sweven grows smaller and smaller – we fly up
and up, changed by rebecoming. Insight feathers,
fettered in a broom closet for too long, become
atrophied. I flap harder in my phantasy.

Nuance *SQUAWKS*, don't give up, give up, change
your thinking, thinking. Fly up to your higher self!
Allow her to come to you! To you!

Sputter-flutter, sputter-flutter, wonky fledgling flight.

SQUAWK! Nuance screeches, this is not a trope!
Healing comes from the future, the future, comes
from the future!

For the first time in eons I breathe, breathe.
I feel each of my feathers open as I spread

my wings to receive the updraft of my higher
self – the feathers hold me – they take me up
and I fly, I fly.

Wings from the island of O – Che and I
learned the ways of the wind, the lingo
of neap tide, heard slack water blue voices
zing with spirit.

Nuance wails, I'm so high I can't feel my beak!
I'm higher than a lawn chair attached to an air
balloon. Look! A slow mo bank to the left, right!
WOOOOOHOOOOO!

Such a strong soaring body, his tail feathers trail
beauty banner. I follow the updraft to match him.
We jet stream laugh lines across the sky.

To reach the isle of O – Che and I crossed estuary
waters – which both connect and separate.

Look, I'm gliding without a care, at one with the air.
You should too! You should too, Lily!

Che and I traversed the waters of the sound,
the in-between, neither here, nor there, we
scaled eternity's edge, 'til it disappeared.

Hyp-na-go-gia! *Hypnagogia!* Nuance heralds.

At one with the sky and with him, I yell back,
I'm inside a mythological cosmology!

And then, we reappeared in a new dimension.

Nuance's voice cracks, *HOICKHOICK!* Look I'm a bird,
he chortles! A plane. I'm a super parrot!

And that's where Che and I tied the knot
on Midsummer Night's Eve, our pockets
full of rings.

Look! I'm a polychromatic golden eagle!
WOOOOOHOOOOO!

You are my beautiful bird friend, Nukey!

It was at the eye of the stone
at the standing stones,

the eye of the stone, with a hole
cut clear through its heart,
that is where we tied the knot.

At the eye of the stone,
the alter stone standing in the centre
of standing stones the bell tolled,
it tolled, for our union.

And it was there, in the in-between
of the Sun rising and setting, that magic
took hold,

on the threshold where shadows speak
and stories are told and untold, we joined
hearts, Che and I.

And the waters shared themselves
with the gleaming fishes and birds
of every kind filled the skies.

Nuance shrieks, don't get caught in the cross-
wind of simultaneous time. *SQUAWK!*

The true could never be truer! I answer.

Dream pons danced in and around us,
as the sun disappeared between pillar
stones, and sank into the ground, and the earth
hummed and the moon rose above seven
tribes of giants from seven continents.

SQUAWK! Watch out for flying burble! Burble!

He makes me laugh. The sky strokes my face
and the warmth of morning sun.

They say, stones still speak to those who wish
to listen, and we wished to listen. Memory nested
in memory.

Nuance hoots, brace yourself, hurly-burly
whirly twirly, incoming, *WOOOOHOOOOO!*

Apparently, no more flying backwards
to go forwards! I climb...

Nuance sings, oh yeah, I'm in-flappable,
I win every single game. I'm unflappable,
so powerful, I'm so fantastical, I'm almost
flapptastical! *WOOOOHOOOOO!*

All thoughts cast off. I'm gone to the great
beyond. Nuance and I mind-combine, click
into telepathy frequency, 111 Hz,

we fly in concert, mirror each other
like a couple of buskers street miming,
only we're not glued to the ground,

our wings open and we soar the skies, blue
as butterflies, lifted on a sound,

we decorate the welkin with a giant figure-
eight – two sides of a great lemniscate,
as we astrogate aerially, our feathers bathed
in morning light,

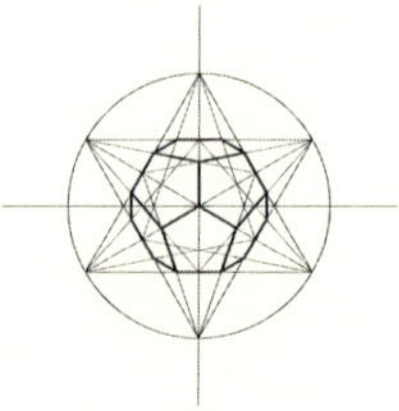

sailing through each others' hues, tying
the shoes of our imaginations together,

mine slipstream red, and Nuances' blue,
together we draw purple lines across
the sky anew, supra-sensorial etch a sketch,

and somehow, amid the depths of uncharted
mystery, an endless knot of lucidity appears,

and releases me from emotions that kept
me bound to memories of loss and time,

and the ions of the air reorder my cells
and my sinew, bone, blood, nerves
and my tissue,

high in the sky I metamorphosis,

and all my wish lists are suddenly found
at the bottom of endless wells, Oubliettes,
axis anima mundi.

Nuance cackles, you found the key! Cockleshells,
eevy, ivy, over here, Lily bird!

Rain's Data Log

Private Notes XXXI – Embranglement

Oh yeah, here it is in my right pocket.

Vexed! Need the black Pearl to rescue us.
Rub the Gad. Code red. *Code red. Jet! Jet!*
Nothing.

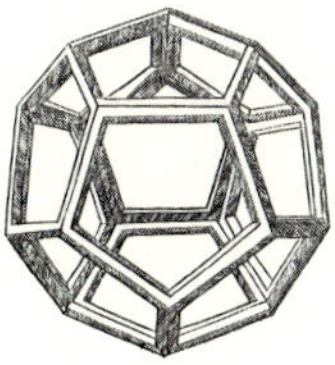

Gauge quizzes, "Is that a dodecahedron?"

"Yes. It's connected to Jet and the Ovoid, but seems it ran out of juice. Guess we're driving Ruin to our own ruin. No matter where we go, they'll hunt us down."

"That's where we are. We'll figure this out! Where there's a will—"

I cut him off, "—there's a dead person!"

He answers, "On the bright side, we'll meet our demise as eleutheromaniacs," then asks, "What's an Ovoid?"

Before I have time to answer, the wind gusts and we swerve sideways. Can hardly keep Ruin our intrepid space chariot, on the road. I white knuckle the wheel and drive hard!

He yells, "We must defy cataclysmic arithmetic. Negative results. Unexplained phenomenon."

"Shite! The ghost car's gaining on us!" Darknet! "They're right up our ass! Can't outrun them."

Gauge repositions himself to see backwards,
"The friggin' thought police are about to— "
SMASH! "—into us! What the fuck?!"

The Gad flies. With a great feat of dexterity
Gauge catches the dodecahedron mid-air.

I yell, "This is a whole new level!
Do you see that?"

"What?"

"In front of us. Coming up. That black Pearl
in the distance."

"It looks like a giant black dot off the side
of the mountain?"

"Ovoid transport. Jet sent it. We have to take it."

"Wait. What are you doing? It's off the side of
the mountain!"

"Hang on. We're about to drive where no aliens
have gone before... "

"Wait... no... not off the cliff... "

Notebook of LM
Entry XVI – Maiden Flight Underwing

Indefinite timeframe. Turn to Nukey, perched
on top of the ancient petroglyph stone and say,
wow, could've been a moment or a terasecond.
Incredible. We were held in the air for forever.

TRILL! Flying on borrowed time.

Yes, and then what a silken landing.

TRILLTRILLTRILL! Indelible memory, Lily!
You look like a giant fey.

Love living in the rainforest. I can breathe here.
My fish wings know how to detach themselves from
my shoulderblades and they do so effortlessly,
they float themselves to the mossy ground.

I scoop them up, wink at Nukey and start back
to The Clove.

He flaps ahead. Over his wing, he screams,
race ya! He loves to win, already has a head start.

I shout to him, first one to The Garlic Clove gets
fresh strawberries! And I sprint in the opposite
direction, privy to shortcuts through the trees.

Can't shapeshift, or leave the wings behind,
just have to run, grey fox, take a left at the Y
branch. Out of breath, I reach the clearing
and screech to a grinding halt—

frozen in chara

theophanic chimera

hold my breath
fragile as opaque glass

this moment of
beauty binds me

it's as if I see it and don't
at the same time

my mind is reborn
my pulse stops

if I breathe
I could shatter perfection
viva
stay in the wow of the now

viva apnea
vivisculpture
the most virtuosic picture

ever not painted,

ΑΘΕ, the high priestess of Sweven
is stretched out on the Erratic Rock,

naked, soaking up the sun, she
wavers between mortal and wolf,

riveted by a single strand of rain,
I forfeit the race and yield to beauty.

On the Erratic, beside ΑΘΕ,
also basking numinous in the sun,
is a gold Scarabaeus.

Am I floating awake or falling asleep?
Realms overlap all over the map,
I am a visitation in this incubation.

A jillion eggs from various creatures,
in a cornucopia of colours rise
to the surface of this consciousness,

some stand upright on the Erratic,
others float in the air, fishlike.

Reality check. The Ouroboros is there.
This is not a fish!

Don't want to disturb her extreme ataraxy.

I tiptoe across the tightrope of her silence,

gently whisper... A... Θ... E...

Yelp! She jumps out of her skin, growls, what!
The surreal illusion evanesces.

I didn't hear you approach!

Sorry! I say, I was in stealth mode, in the middle
of a foot and flight race with Nuance.

She springs to the ground spry, exulting, Lily,
you could get seriously injured sneaking up
on me like that!

Her eyes widen and her pupils dilate lupine
until she spies my wings and switches her
mood. With a sparkle in her eyes she says,
did you do it? You did it. Good for you!

Yes! And I should have returned your call, but
I got caught in the excitement of it all. That said,
I just took the wings out for a flight with Nukey!
And I did it, ΑΘΕ, I flew like I used to, at one
with the wind as the sun rose gold on the edge
of the sublime.

Eximious! She wraps herself in a cozy towel, says
I'm elated. She slides into her flipflops, adding,
I need to talk to you about something.

After yesterday's news and the Rh-null blood
connection, I'm afraid of what she might say.

Sit down, she says. I slide onto the Erratic beside
her. It's warm from the sun. She continues, slowly,
we've learned that Rain and Che share the exact
same DNA and RNA.

Dread falls out the bottom of my being.

With sensitivity ΑΘΕ says, I know it's verging
on noumenon. When we made the discovery,
I was addlepated, so I validated and revalidated.
Lily, I've pondered every possible explanation
and my only conclusion leads to one question,
is it possible Che had a twin?

A twin! I say, no! I need a moment to process.
I'm reeling, gutted, having trouble breathing,
my airways feel blocked. I can't talk.

She murmurs, hold onto the rock to stabilize.
You can't afford to fall. Take your time, Lily.

My life's unravelling. Is it retrograde?

Drink some of this gingerroot iced tea, here,
and hold my jade amulet for a minute. Find
balance.

Thank you. Yes. Balance. Barnacles! The thing is,
Che WAS adopted. She told me when she tried
to find her birth mother. I continue, it's possible,
but what are the chances?

Prolonged pause.

Sorry ΑΘΕ, but I feel cosmically blindsided. Wow.
This is a lot to take in. The way Che disappeared,
the loss of my O-naut, trying to retrieve it. WOW.
And now Rain. I feel like I'm on the verge of a—

ΑΘΕ comforts me.

I croak out, if Che is Rain's twin, then it's likely
Rain is a full-fledged Oneironaut as well.

Time distils into a tight knot,
            into the single droplet
                            of an extract tincture.

I say, remember when we bottled the essence
of our fishes when we slept at high altitudes?

Yes

        we could use them right now

                            if you'd like

      time   hangs   onto

        the air   for dear   life

tries to survive becomes

a cloud of irrelevance

which loiters between us

AΘE attempts to ground the moment. She says, my immediate concern is for Rain and the danger she poses to herself. You know more than anyone what happens when the amygdala floodgate opens and the undiluted Oneironaut breaks loose.

Shellfish! I'm fit to be tied! If she receives the entire motherload download at once as I did, her whole unconscious psyche could completely unravel before it transforms into free radical.

AΘE adds, not to mention the existential threat posed by the DOD.

Not good. This is not good at all, I concede, sorry I let her leave.

Not on you, we all summoned her here, cadendo crescimus. And it was important for her to return.

Non cadere procidens!

AΘE splices, I believe she's the O-naut catalyst we've been waiting for. For change.

I shake my head; we better beware the second coming of that which shall not be mentioned. Nothing changes.

AΘE agrees, and I won't mention the emperor's new clothes, as a transparent hoax.

I don't overstate when I say, she's in grave danger.

Take heart. Jet will guide her in, keep her safe.
And as per our gathering, her friend, Gauge,
is now travelling with her.

Make sure they're not followed, but bring them
back to Sweven alive. We should probably use
the filling station tunnel. I'll be at the beehive
for the next bit, after that, at the distillery.

Achcha! Make the strongest elixir ever!
We're going to need it!

Will do. Here's to the goldest wildflower honey-
bee wine ever. Our spirits will reach 190 Proof!

Boom! She licks her fingertip and sweeps it be-
neath my chin, a time-honored ritual of the stage.
At once, she murmurs, merde, sidestepping
the superstition of saying good luck.

I smile and quip; may the hand of fate speak
the language of water.

Rain's Data Log

Private Notes XXXII – Mortiferous Fulmination

We hit the bend at max speed. Gauge yells,
"Oh no! We're going to hit max air—!"

I fly Ruin off the cliff pointed in the direction
of the Pearl. We both scream, "Whoa!!!!!!"
SOS! Help us, Jet!

*Jet: I'm teleporting you for the last time! After this,
I'm out! Going dark.*

PING! We slingshot into the black Pearl. Ruin
is gone. Gauge and me float in Ovoid space. *[t=0]*

Still holding the hubcap, Gauge exults, "Yes!
That was a miraculous leap! What the hell?
Where are we?"

"I'll explain this later. Right now, we have to stay
in the moment to survive, so we don't get cremated
alive." For an instant I breathe safe in liminal space.

Then... *ZZZST ZZZST* "Owww! What the—?"

ZZZST ZZZST "Owww!" We both get zapped.

Gauge yells, "I'm guessing this is not supposed
to happen?"

"No! It's a first! Jet warned me about the Ovoid-
bends but I'm guessing it was the only way she
could shake us free of the DOD!"

"Free to be tortured?"

"No."

"These negative charges are super intense. We won't be able to withstand them much longer."

Jet! Help! Jet! What is going on!? We're being tased, stunned by anvil zaps electromagnetic. *ZZZST ZZZST*

Gauge joins, "It's some kind of gravitational collapse, a bad synapse snap, event horizon gone wrong. This Pearl's a live wire! *ZZZST ZZZST*

ZZZST We both yelp, "Owwww!"

"We're astronauts floating in a vacuum at zero-g, getting brutalized by inner space."

"Or argonauts being battered by outer space!"

I add, "Or, we're free radical Greeks in search of the Golden Fleece?"

"It's a whole new level of storm chasing, Rain, we're literally part of the storm itself," Gauge surmises.

"We're ice nuclei in a terrestrial cocktail mixer of a solar superstorm. I never imagined this." *ZZZST ZZZST*

ZZZST "Ouch! Or could've imagined!"

I rally, "Maybe we're part of something larger, more a G-5 geomagnetic astrocyclone – a gravity well of dark matter tempest, an ugly quantum weather anomaly." *ZZZST ZZZST*

"Yow! Each zap's more excruciating than the... autoimmune! Obviously larger than simulated live action chasing." *ZZZST*

Jet! Help! Red alert! Red alert! I speculate, "Maybe we're micro-components of a whole that's killing itself."

"My mind's white knuckling, hanging onto reality so tight I can't seem to get a grip!" *ZZZST ZZZST*

"The absolute sound is the birth of infinity. Wish we were indestructible Tardigrades."

"Yay, Tardigrades." *ZZZST* "Ouch!"

Jet! Red alert! SOS!

<<<<<<<can't help much longer>>>>>>>

M

Yow!

H 1 is H_2

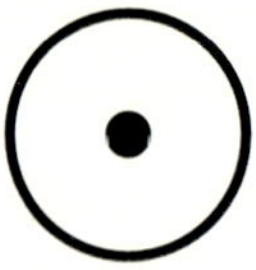

<<<<<<<can't hold on>>>>>>>

"Hold tight Gauge! There's nothing we can do!"

"Will do. Not in the mood to die today!"

Wonder what happens when you die in a fish?

Three Runes turned to the Empyrean—
Thurisaz ᚦ
Sowilo ᛊ
Laguz ᛚ

the seven Willows of Sweven
stand united around a large fishing net,
which extends in a circle in front of The Clove,

they mend the mesh, knot the knots,
pull weaving needles in and through
holes, while they sing to the sun

3 5 7 9

4 6 8

< < < < < < <i am almost done> > > > > > >

at once they hear the plea and stop
astrolaters, time suspends skyward

they know – a foolish fish,

frightened by the noise, may rouse
a false awakening, and the fisher will then
be caught in the infinite loop
of disillusionment,

the Willows return to their song
only this time, a euphonious paean chant

tacit and yet collectively conscient
of what they have heard

Divination Invocation
ᚲᚢᚨᚲᛖ ᚦᛖ ᛖᚱᚦ ᚨᚹᚨᚲᛖ

Netting the Bee Key

(All)
We whirr, whirr,
amplify our frequency,
lift soundwaves to 111 Hz.

We summon Terra Mama Serpent
to quake the embryo of Rain awake, awake,
to allow her O-naut to break free
of its shell, so she might become
the true salamander she was meant
to be. It's only when you embody
your wandering spirit that you
become your whole self.
Ring the bell. Ring the bell.
Fisher be free.
PING!

(AΘE)
Rain must sever ties with old realities,
simultaneously, we must
protect her comrade.
Serpent of old. Serpent of new.

(All)
Yes-s-s-s-s-s-s!!!
We snip the navel chord
corkline combined, so Rain might sail
the skies of fish, umbilical free.
Williwaw.

(Jet)
Cut the chord between a usurper's
subjugation and Ovoid electrocution.

(All)
Yes-s-s-s-s-s-s!!!
Together, we call upon divine
illumination, to sever the despotic tether,
together we alchemize diamonds out of nets.

In times of stress and healing
one must slow the heartbeat
to standstill. The Willows exhale.
Silence.

The entire net eclipses, it flashes electric,
lotus blue for an instant.

(Keiron)
Embody truth but do not know it.
Summon the spirit of fire!

The net is bioluminescent between them
as they cluster, in a flash it becomes
an electric lotus blue spinneret.

(All)
Yes-s-s-s-s-s-s!!!
The net speaks, inspired,
for the tectonic shift that lifts
DOD maleficence and delivers prime
matter to the house of clay, to be fired.

ᛈᚨᛊᛏ ᛚᛁᚷᚺᛏᚾᛁᛜ ᛊᛏᛟᚱᛗᛊ
PING!

Another flash sees a glimpse into another
realm. The net drops its disguise.
It is. It is not a fish catcher.

(Jet)
Our collective dream has dwindled.
Days are numbered, moments are few.

(Agate-Nyx)
May the flames of salamander
awaken, bring Rain and Gauge to us.

(Lily)
ᛈᚱᛟᛏᛖᚲᛏᛟᚾ ᚹᛟᚱ ᚱᚨᛁᚾ

Reality restored, we pull and loop,
the net, to refocus our minds.

I speak through the needle
held between my teeth.

Anam Cara. Remember when
Che told me she was vegan.

The Willows titter. I knew I'd get
them to follow me. They shake
their heads, needles burrow.
I continue,

it was the first dinner we held
in her honour after she arrived here
and she said she was vegan, so we only
made enough salmon for six.

All Willow eyes dance with amusement,
imbued with the individualistic recollection

Yes! It was the 1st feast of the 1st council
of the Willows and Che held out her plate
for a piece of salmon.

I said, you said you were vegan,
and she said, I'm vegan
but I eat salmon.

And the way she looked to me
was the way I looked to her,

and in that glimmer, we changed
time as time changed us, evergreen.

I said, a pescatarian vegan?
Yes, was her answer.

In real time the Willows sigh
between holes. I lower my head
and add, salmon are anadromous.

Bisous Θ axioms, so are Oneironauts.

I murmur to the Willows and it was then,
in that eyeblink spark, that Che and I
awakened and we knew one another.

Anam Cara.

Our netting comes to a standstill. A prolonged
silence intervenes. A wave of grief trembles
through the Willows.

Jet bromides, friends, with the patience it takes
to weave sound fishnets, let us summon multitudes
of orisons for Rain & Gauge to unwaveringly reach
the safehouse, and then let us create pons to guide
them forward through our complex underground.

ΑΘΕ asks, how's Rain's nous?

Jet sighs, very tenuous, the DOD hacked the Pearl, causing intense interference, which has resulted in what seems to be a new strain of Ovoid-bends.

No!

Yes! I'd equate this iteration with being pressed up against an electric fence soaking wet. Terrible electrical zapping.

Hive concern.

Everyone, I'm just trying to hold myself together and get them home here in one piece.

AΘE cautions, we must guard Rain as if our lives depended upon it, because they do.

Someone adds, and Gauge.

AΘE nods and murmurs, my dear Willows, there's a crucial message I must impart to you.

It's almost as though the net no longer exists.

AΘE persists, it has recently been brought to our attention, that Rain is indeed an Oneironaut.

Sound waves flatten. Silence falls to 0 decibels.

And there's more, she says, we have now verified that Rain is indeed twin sister to Che.

Audible gasp.

Jet cuts into the fracture, back to the field report, the DOD were closing in on R & G, so I was forced to O-teleport them to the Frontier.

ΑΘΕ says, what about the Ovoid-bends?

Jet advises, it won't be a comfortable ride, but it's my belief we can get them away from immediate danger. Tomorrow, after they get some shut eye, will be more difficult, as they embark on the most dangerous part of their journey thus far. Forced to proceed by foot, they'll be mostly on their own. I will try to guide them through the dark entities who lurk in the Sylcanor Forest.

Chorus of gasps. Prolonged silence.

ΑΘΕ treads lightly, there was a time the old growth forest was the safest place on earth. Now it's riddled with DOD Oneiroi Daemons, and any person who wanders into those parts is instantly exterminated.

Jet sweeps her long blue hair aside, revealing tragus helix and lobe piercings – whimsical techno-geek. She adds, I know everything seems harrowing right now.

The good news is, although Rain doesn't know it, she's in full fish-bloom. True, she's not in control of her powers yet, but I think she'll be in O-neurosync soon. That said, I'm still able to speak to her in fish with my Pythia self.

ΑΘΕ spins it, let it be a mighty journey, Willows. This is the end of the beginning.

A twisting and turning triquetra knot rises up out of the net and floats between them. They sing.

(All)
Ahhhhh, beloved,
let Rain regain the full range
of her O-naut and without getting caught
let her and Gauge return
to Sweven.

Guarded by the Serpent
and the Secret Order of Oneironauts.

Let it be.

(three claps)

δ θ γ

In spirit we go.

They raise their arms toward the floating
triquetra. The three interwoven arcs
unwind themselves, like violet ribbons,

the segments unfurl and subtly rotate
into spirally curls

until the violet ribbons
transform into a rose gold triskelion.

In unison the Willows
snap their fingers. The holy shape bursts
into red-hot sparks
which rain down on them
and the blue net.

PING!

THE BUREAU
DEPARTMENT OF DREAMS
SECURITY INTELLIGENCE REPORT
CODE RED—MOST WANTED

File: 210178MS5H
Date/Time: Future Perfect Tense
Subject: Rain (ID # 220 455 816)

ESCALATED VIOLATION REPORT:
Armed & Dangerous.
Travelling in No-go Zone.

RECOMMENDATION:
Emergency Alert.
Apprehend Immediately. Alive.

_______________*below the bottom line*_______________

Office of Dr. Lester Maggott, inside The Bureau. Maggott sits behind his palatial desk smoking a cigar.

Maggott is surrounded by secret service agents and bots. Shelly attempts to gain respect by standing at attention with her arms obediently locked behind her back.

Maggott roars, "What is your problem!? She's one little insignificant mouse. Are you telling me a meagre science rodent managed to escape X-City and is now somehow on the lam? How is that scenario even possible?

You imbeciles! Catch this insipid little dissident NOW, or it's the end of your line. You'll be stripped of positions and branded treasonous."

The agents and bots systematically and uniformly exit Maggott's office, leaving him alone with Shelly.

"And as for you! I want # 799 brought to her proverbial knees! Do you hear me, Shelly!? I want this Che bitch to hear nothing but a shrill hum, at a frequency so calculated it embeds itself into the very fabric of her innermost thoughts and memories for hours until her mind literally caves, 'til it fractures. And when it does, I want her screams of resistance heard all the way to the outer borders of X-City. Do you understand me, Shelly? Up the ante x 10.

This is not merely torture, it's a recalibration of her mind and memories. It is a demonstration of power and a reminder that under my rule, extreme dream and disobedience will not be tolerated."

Rain's Data Log

Private Notes XXXIII – Fish Out of H2O

PING! We swirl down the psychotropic drain,
the surreality of noir uncertainty, in slow mo
our bodies spill through a tenebrous sky, free
of the black Pearl, both yelling, "whoa!!!"

We're a microgravitational anomaly, cascading
into the eye of oblivion.

Gauge echoes in the whirligig, "The bottom of
an Aeon just fell out, invisible as the magnetic
meridian! We're caught in an infinite loop
hole, aero to astro-nautical at the speed of light,
we're spinning in a vacuum."

We're mulmul plummeting, jettisoned by a way-
ward waft. *[c]*

It is. It is not.

A curate's egg, *clueless as stardust FOOSH.*

I alight, feather frequency, in a perfect faceplant
slow mo into the dirt. I look up from ground level,
squint through silt *FLASH* of unfathomable gold,
orichalcum maybe. Where am I? *Where am I not?*

I'm an ultraterrestrial in a wasteland dust bowl,
echo of the abyss *HISS'N'ZAP.* Look alive, Sunrise.

I surmise with my Dragonfly eyes I'm somewhere
in the middle of nowhere's demise, like falling into
the twilight zone without a ray gun,

elucidating in the distance behind clouds of detritus
is a timeworn neon sign blitzing out on its last leg,
it's fizzling out *BLINKBUZZ* strobing an eerie boonish
warning in morse code *BLINKBUZZ.*

The Frontier *BUZZ* **Motel.**

A dire place with an omni-proximity to creepy,

I drag myself up, brush myself off gasping and
inch towards the motel entrance quivering,
"Gauge?"

Each footfall is more disturbing than the last.
This is the middle earth of quasi-eternity, only
way worse. "Gauge! Where the frack are you?"
Can't see him anywhere.

Hair-trigger, torn. On one hand I'm exhausted,
need a room to sleep, on the other, I don't want
to go inside, one more, *where the heck is G-man?*

Need somewhere to hideout, take cover. Jet must
have landed us here for a reason. Just do it, go in.
Don't do it. Don't go in. No! Don't not go in.

It is. It is not.

A functioning motel? Can't see inside the check-in-
check-out windows – obscured by a film of mildew.
I open the door, instantly overwhelmed by an awful
stench and a requiem to the lost plays in my mind.
Wish Gauge would materialize. Walk in.

Standing lifeless still, behind a worm-eaten reception
desk is a nasty piece of work, who I mind-name,
Mr. Lost Frontier.

Act unfazed, just another day in the neighborhood, must appear unshrinking.

He leers at me from behind beady little rat-eyes, half of his mouth forms a sinister smile, the other a seething sneer. No teeth but he still looks blood-thirsty. *EEK!* Vampire, no, a zombie.

Soundtrack kicks in: Psycho-killer knife stabbing.

Pinned to the peeling wallpaper behind Mr. Lost is a chain of decaying signs, or yellowing eyesores, which read – No Refunds, Smoking Allowed, Enter at Your Own Risk – proving clichés are not a joke.

Without batting an eye, I slide my cash across the great divide *[0° latitude]* concealing the wad with my sleight of hand, to cloak from hidden surveillance cams.

Narrowing his eyes at me, he hands me an old-skool key, "Number 13."

No. If the final gavel drops you a life sentence, you must remain deadpan. Yes, cool as a crisper cucumber, I say, "Thank you," and I split.

As I make my way to lucky #13, I whisper to myself, "Gauge where are you?"

This is happening. *This is not happening.*

Jet? Where the hell is Gauge!? Last time I saw him he was spilling through space.

Yes, this is definitely not an exemplary vacancy, the fleabag Inn, likely a fish bait motel to capture fleeing fishers.

Truth known, hearing Uncle E's stories, I always wondered what it would be like outside X-City, *beyond The Grille.* "Gauge? Gauge! Where are you?"

Uncle Ed would tell me about escaping and being free and I'd imagine seedy motels & manual type-writer's in his stories. Miss him so much. When he called me his *rebus dingbat*, I felt like the original emoji.

Egads! The light fell so fast. It's so dark I can't see the damn numbers and I'm seriously starting to get worried. Where the frack is Gauge? "Gauge, are you out there?"

Why do we sense more in the dark? Why do I hear and fear more?

Where's that stupid unlucky door, #13. They say, the sensor receptors of our tastebuds become amplified in the darkness.

Uncle E said, before the time of curfews, he'd drive out of X-City and park in the middle of nowhere in the pitch dark and he'd recline supine on the roof of his car to stargaze at the stars for hours to locate himself in the galaxy. That's what he said.

Because of Uncle Ed, I'd picture what it was like on the outside and he introduced me to videos of nature and trains and ships and storms and quirky trivia.

Lucky #13 and still no Gauge. Click, ease the door open. *Whoa!* Hit by a pungent waft of cadaverine.

Gag! Chock! For some reason my ears pop.

I just have to believe he's going to show up.

This place is a nightmare dump! Close the door behind me.

It's still hard to imagine that ancient artists drew pictures of elephants from verbal descriptions.

Notebook of LM
Entry XVIII – Fixing Rain Catchers

Shumba, Violet, do you want to come? They both jump at the chance of going somewhere and they don't even care where.

I tell them, today we'll finish the Rain catchment on The Hive. If there's time, we'll change the socks on the other four tanks. The copasetic canines follow.

When I perform routine tasks, it gives my mind time to catch up to what I'm actually thinking. Had to retrain my brain, because I used to process in fish-time.

On the bright side, this way I get my chores done and it gives me a chance to confer with my tail wagging therapists. The Hive's really coming along, isn't it? They take their places on the stoop to sun, ignoring my soliloquizing,

you know, there was a time divine, eons ago, when I'd look into fossiliferous stones to see the future and to listen to their song.

I check the rain gauge. It's amazing. The levels have remained inside optimum range. Can't tell if my confidants are listening. Under my breath I whisper,

that was back when I travelled across thresholds seamlessly and went on Oneironaut adventures, ovum-to-ovum into the abraxas of dream fish.

Back when cosmogeny was more than an idea,
I would try to harmonize with the mysteries
of the universe, omni-to-omni and otherwise.
Mental note aloud, tomorrow, I'll fit the down-
spouts with leaf guards. Tediously unfun.

Once upon a time when surveillance capitalism
meant personalized consumption, smart privacy
piracy, yes, before the dominance of algorithms
and oligarchies.

I remember those times, before hardlines were drawn
between people, before the great divide between rich
and poor became a chasm no one could cross.

Like any good pawapist their listening is interspersed
with the odd *uh-huh*. On a riff, I continue, yes,

that was before the new world 'odor' re-ordered us
in their own image for their personal gain, before
they realized they could phish our fishes and sell
our secrets and our identities back to us.

Shumba grumbles. I'm disturbing his fish. Wonder
if I'm his pet in the other realm. I talk like no one's
listening – because they're not. I rant on,

that was back before the DOD used free speech
to quash free speech, thinker beware, menticide
presides.

I slide the sock over the opening to catch debris
as it flows out of the spout. It's a perfect fit. Feel
a moment of personal pride, before I'm hit
with the sadness of knowing we are no longer
permitted to fish or even make a wish.

The entire Morpheus-sphere has become censored, dry as a sun-brittle bone. Myths have become lost stories, as have our history and we are forbidden from prophesizing, or recognising what is clear water.

Right, water. That's what I need.

Hey you guys, let's go for a swim!

Rain's Data Log

Private Notes XXXIV – Deep Into the Dive

Not even a burner cell to call Gauge. Damn it!
Starting to freak out. Feel like a lost home
page. Where? Where the hell is he? *Jet?*
Are you out there?

Wedge a derelict chair under the doorknob,
remove the dead bedspread caked in lust-crust,
roll it into a ball and ditch it in the corner.

Gag! Crikey. Crush. Don't need to comb the room
for crumbs of creepiness, ubiquitous noxiousness.

Uncle Ed limned, always do a motel crevice check.
Oh no, the crevice check. Slide my hand between
the flaccid mattress & boxspring, *damn!*

I exhume a crumpled centrefold from, *oh no,* dry
heave. Where has this been? Hurl in my mouth.
Swallow. Can't. Tears get ensnared in my larynx,
they gag me burked.

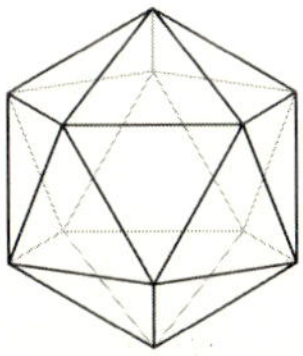

Retch, I feel something else, hope it's not a porn
ball! *Darknet!* When I uncrumple the crumpled
wad,

I discover a Great Icosahedron made of platinum,
archaically orichalcum, hidden in the middle of
the crinkly lechery.

I'm beginning to think, when I think something,
it happens. Better be careful what I think.

Egads! There're cigarette burns and bloodstains
all over the pillowcases, both skanky and spooky
combined. *Spanky.*

At this point, I can't even mask my disgust
behind a reusable face. Can't avoid exposure,
if I squeezed myself into a hazmat skin. *Mercy!*

I've been grottified! Slide the Icosahedron inside
my pocket next to the Gad and lie down on top
of the sheets with my clothes on, disposable armor.
Tie my hoody around my face, this place puts
the scuzz back in scuzzy. Goodnight disgrace.

Can't sleep. This place is an insomniac's worst
nightmare. Would rather wander than wallow.

Pace the place, already a threadbare path. Stop.
Peak out the window, sill littered with fly corpses.
A gnarly boneyard of summer exoskeletons.

Where's Gauge? Don't see anything! All is quiet
in the heart of skankiness. Seems we weren't tailed.
Ovoid officially defective.

Need to see things as they are not as I'd like them
to be, gotta cut out the sugar coating. Or maybe,
I should see things as they aren't. *Not!*

Anything to avoid waking-up dead – strangled
to death in my sleep by a Frontier excarnationist.

I won't know I'm not awake if I don't know
I'm already dead. And what about Gauge. No,
I'd feel it in my bones.

But if he is dead then I'm next. Yes, and I'll be discovered, my boney hands tied to a jammed steering wheel, windows locked, me trapped in the drivers' seat at the bottom of an abysmal lake, thalassophobic.

My thoughts are deafening, can't hear myself think.

They're so loud the DOD can probably hear them all the way to X-City and they're likely listening to them right now, thought tracking me.

I know, I'll blast the anachronistic TV to drown out noetic noise. *Damn!* I have no idea how to turn this antiquated TV on. Noise begets noise begets, a nasty fever.

Maybe this twisty knobby dial will turn it on.

Notebook of LM
Entry XIX – Timelapse Tide

dogs on the beach sitting on shoreline
stones – watching me swim, as lookouts,
guardians, Shumba and Violet

hold my breath and swim laps of the sea
with the hope I'll bring a morsel of fish
back to me – to swing forward, to throw
me back

to hallowed times, littoral to the strand,
to my other mind, swim back and forth
to go forth

kicking wild, arm over arm to reach the crack
in the door, I crawl toward the gravity of hope,
for all that I lost, stroke after stroke, to cope
with the idea I may never return
to myself

intrinsic

when fish breathed through me
and I through them, past realistic,
unrealistic, into the astonishing

hold my breath and swim laps of the sea,
longing to reach the edge of blanking out,
going for broke
crawling the current of destiny

mutiny across the tide crest 'til I reach
the fine line and cross over to that mysterious
ocean of little stars, divine delirium lights,
replacing one kind of sight with another
to coming to and moving from

at once, the Judgement card and its reverse,
self-doubt beyond redemption, a broken curse,
splashing and gasping
                    past letting go or holding on
                    simply
                    a brief glimpse of eternity

before it too is gone
and I all that is left is for me
to float along
empty to the sea

Rain's Data Log

Private Notes XXXV – Fishing for Answers

Forever ago, I hit the wall of eldritch
and my world came sliding down. *[*$_{76}$*Os]*

I thought I was escaping, instead I was trapped
getting zapped orphic in the Ovoid.

At some point we crossed over Kármán's line,
where the earth ends and space begins – we were
caught in a vortex spin.

Can't breathe. Stop. Can't stop. Go. Can't go. Full
stop! *Period.*

What am I going to do? *Can't move forward without
Gauge. I'm stuck. Cripes!* I never get anything right.
Not good enough. Enough, is never enough.

Nothing is impossible

is nothing impossible

is nothing nothing?

Impossible.

Nought.

*Right! How do I control my fish when fish don't even
exist?* Are fish chasing me or am I chasing them?

There must be markers. Yes! Biomarkers always
tell the truth. *Do they?* Yes, they do. *Not. What?
What's truth?* No such thing. *True.* Not. Round

and round we go – on a roundabout of circular reasoning.

I know that the invisible code living inside me speaks more about me than what I know about myself. Now that's true. *But who wins?* No one, ever! *Well, if that's true, then there's no such thing as a loser.* Good, I'm protected!

What I do know is – if I get caught its curtains, game over for real. *I'm a starfish.* No, a jellyfish. *In that case I'll leave no markers, no sign I was ever here – no skeleton to inter.*

And what's up with Jet? *I don't get it.* Sometimes she's here, and sometimes she's not. It's like she's the accelerator key. *No, I think she's an auditory hallucination.* And who's that other garrulous voice inside my head.

This is a mind-boggling maelstrom, a neuro-divergences' worst nightmare!

$Zn+1 = Zn^2 + C$

PSYCHIC ACCELERATOR

In the mist-laden groves of Delphi, I'm standing before Pythia, who vacillates between her woman & serpent selves. We lock eyes. She remains snake on top of what appears to be the omphalos stone.

I think I'm my Rain self to learn about her Python self. Her green eyes hypnotize.

Inviting and intimidating, she slides in & out of sunset shades, but she has a super chill vibe, & I like her calming effect.

I hope this isn't the aurora where I meet my darkness.

She knows I know she knows my scent. Slowly I move towards her, mirroring her raw sinew.

I align yourself with the rhythms of the grove, for it is her grove & the pillars & olive trees. Reach out my hand.

Her body powerful. Sensations grow. Her song reverent. She flicks her tongue. Untamed silence in understanding she moves her body onto mine. Strangely fluid. Eyes ethereal.

We intertwine around the energies of centuries, ancient forces coil. Our skin is smooth it slides. Hers is silky to my fingertips.

I hiss her on the flicks. In low tones, I speak sotto, "When you take away the fishes of a people there's nothing for them to aspire to,

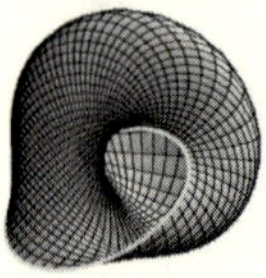

∵ even if they know something's egregiously amiss, they can't seem to put our finger on it, powerless to stop the hiccups, no matter how long they hold their breath. Will you help me shed the darkness that lives inside my serpent heart."

She hisses, "They know it, but don't want to admit it ∵ if they admit it, they'll have to do something about it."

"Yes, so they stick their head in quicksand, unable to find the root of their own algorithm, in a sense they've lost the thread of themselves."

"There are ways to save yourself & all fishers." She winds herself around my body. I'm the rod of Asklepios. She is remarkably soothing.

Not moving, I say, "Noise begets noise begets hegemonic menticide. I got sucked into the gyre trap. I left X-City & now I have no centre. I'm living, running in the throes of a perpetual nosedive. *[$\propto 2\Omega \times Vo$]*

She moves around me, "You no longer live by State tyranny, threats on threats & promises of Shangri-la, land of honey, or censorship with an info blackout twist, paralyzed for fear they'll land on their most wanted list, total paternalism."

"To quote a book that got burned, 'It was a pleasure to burn.'"

She implores, "I'm almost at the end of my life, Rain. Please listen. The DOD are close to winning, to killing me & all other fishers, including you & Gauge."

"Gauge is a fisher?"

"Yes, a Nox Chieftain. Listen closely, the time bomb's ticking. This will be my last transference. Tomorrow leave before dawn, travel old skool, by foot.

Head west and find the Sylcanor forest. The Icosahedron will glow blue when you're headed in the right direction. It will glow blood red when the Daemons are nigh.

Deep in the mountains beside a lake, find a loom beside a broom which will lead you to a clay pot, where you'll find a potter and a hidden room, safe spot. There, you'll receive an oral parol from a Demiurge."

"But what about Gauge?"

(δ θ γ dream end)

I jolt awake. Sit up in a start.

Is that a mouse trap in the corner?

Death Noodles! Where the hell is Gauge?

Nothing but the silence of Bargain Bin Inn.

Better try to catch
some zzz's,

my head sandwiched
between a septic pillow,

and the jeremiad rumble
of an ill-fated minibar.

Notebook of LM
Entry XX – Plenty of Fish in the Sea

standing on the shoreline watching
waves lapse; more sweep than crash

obsidian time passes

waves lapse, sigh, relapse
collapse into the orphic

one of my most hallowed pass times
to unwind, rewind, overwind,
standing on the shoreline

the serpent winds around my Caduceus
around the desiderium
of my heart

a beauty I'll never leave, o

to breathe the ions of sea,
who is waiting for me
to dive into her again
aquatica

to hold my breath, to stop breathing
until I reach the other side of her
and myself, ahhhhh

a single raindrop
falls from the eye of the sky
and lands on my cheek

what are the chances?
why is the sky so sad?

the droplet rolls down my face ◦
sky clad dyad ◦ teardrop and raindrop
at once ◦ tincture of grief
rolls down my cheek

the sorrow of her shadow from afar
folds into me ◦
her dark cloud rage
her foreboding ◦ her grief

slides into mine
our sadness combines ◦
in a confluence of sorrow

as we feel our way around the darkness
for a spark of light,

we build up our nerve ◦ deep song
in a kind of burning which twists

it turns duende into another woe
as we gather our lightning bolts

and thunder roar
together

about to tear asunder ◦ I don't question why
even for an instant ◦ for we are the squall
we cry and bawl and act out wild
from here

we use the last of our strength
to carry each others' tears ◦

drenched in a tirade of tempest fears

we mingle blue ◦ together

soaked in rage

◦ sluices

sea ◦ of tears

◦ dive in ◦ to the ◦ sea

◦ vul ◦ ner ◦ able ◦ ◦

◦ i n t o

◦ blue ◦ as sky ◦

s k y ◦ o r ◦

◦ o ◦ r ◦ ◦

i ◦ g i ◦ n ◦

i ◦ n ◦ i ◦ n

◦ d ◦ i ◦ ◦

◦ ◦ g ◦ o

◦

<<<<<<<stone echo – echo of stone>>>>>>>

Rain's Data Log
Private Notes XXXVI – Red Sky in Morning

Red sky in the morning, sailors warning, yeah,
why do I know that?

This morning the sky's laser red, fluorescent
with streaks of doom – *a chilling redshift omen*
from an ancient prophecy,

a predictive dawning, better watch out, stay
sharp, it's the visual equivalent of hearing
a fascist propaganda song, sung beautifully,

while lurking in the wings, behind a well-designed
agitprop scrim – is a brat-a-tat-tat militia armed
with machine guns,

pointed directly at civilians gathered in a square,
mesmerized somnambulant by a dulcet serenade.

Before the mass massacre begins and nowhere
to run, s-u-s-p-e-n-s-e

slow
as molasses

and everyone backstage

knows once the radical aria ends
it's lights out – for their fellow citizens

how will they live with themselves

yet everyone's stifled
breathless.

Where did that come from? Swipe that thought.

Must stay in the here and now and look for
Gauge. Gauge! Where are you?

Red sky morning turns my skin neon red inferno,
sensation of sleepwalking – gliding across the post
apocalyptic parking lot, empty as ambivalence,
glowing with foreboding.

Mr. Lost Frontier, likely a sleeper agent, is sleeping
off his intoxicated graveyard shift. If I move swiftly
I can suss out the place. I round the corner, abracadabra,
I sever his access to the outside world.

Look over and there's Gauge, curled up on a lawn chair,
clutching that stupid hubcap. He blinks himself awake,
"Rain, there you are. Couldn't find you after I crash-landed
last night, so I thought I'd sleep here and find you in
the morning."

"I'm so relieved to see you! But right now, we gotta
scram!"

"Okay."

"This way," I say, and we make a run for it through
the Hades sunrise, yes, red sky in the morning fire
pyre. In total we synthesis, we ignite, skin crimson,
become one with the alpenglow. Two flames on
the run. I whisper-yell, "Jet told me which way to go."

We duck into the Sylcanor forest, quiet and unsuspecting
as an intel gathering hot air spy balloon. Gauge has the
hubcap pressed to his chest armor-like. I joke, "don't look
back at No-tell Motel, Orpheus."

He answers, "Okay, Morpheus."

"What, not Eurydice?" We giggle. His laugh is contagious – always makes me smile. His eyes gravitational pull me to the centre of his star.

I check the Great Icos, it's glowing voltaic blue indigo, awe-inspiring and terrifying at the same time, we run for our lives into the wilds, toward the depths of the forest,

to and from obscurity at the same time, my only indemnity is analogous to absurdity, indecipherable as A-Z – I see stars, stars,

my eyes are undivided, *I've heard of the endorphin rush when runners see stars – that's what I'm seeing in this forest full of distorted depth – stars, stars, and more phosphorescent stars. Massive distortions!*

The trees are a wall of prison bars, seeing stars – not used to running – slow down, about to pass out.

Gauge stops, "Sorry, out of shape, have to catch my breath for a second. I'm seeing stars!"

"We must maintain a steady trajectory to not see stars. Look the Icos is indigo, we're headed in right direction. Come on, we got this." *Walk on MacWheezy, walk on.*

To distract him as we hike, I say, "Wonder what's it's called when you lose someone in a graveyard."

"What?"

"You know, when you trudge around in search
of an engraved name on headstone?"

He quizzically responds, "a fool's tomfoolery?"

We twitter, "a ghost hunter's errand."

We walk in silence. That's one of the things I love
about Gauge – our comfort level with shared silence.

We stop. Listen. Take inventory. Shoulder check.
Nothing in our wake. Experiencing being alone
together in the wilds. We always fished of doing
this together – only different. No sign of Daemons,
or red. The forest is verdant in sylvan light.

Wonder how we'll survive. I'm already starving
and in need of a radix-brew. How I am even living
without coffee? Forget it. Walk on.

Breathe in the green and gold morning rays as they
stream photonic through the trees. Check Icos.
Indigo.

The first and last time I was in the trees like this,
I was in Sweven. Sweven. The only other time, I was
with Uncle Ed, who took me on immersive VR experiences.

Everything's alive in this forest. I interrupt the back-
drop, "I spy with my mantis shrimp eyes a googolplex
of watchers without electronic guise."

"Yep. *A TREE(3)* of living things, rife with life." Disk
underarm, we walk on in the direction of indigo.

I say, "Yes, deeper into the morass of a turvy funk,
to get to the other side before we're irreversibly sunk."

"Skunked," he looks at me with merriment.

"Mwahahaha! I love the forest so much I almost forget why we're here."

New levels of thought riot emerge. Gauge propels me from fear-based life into something not yet named.

My blinders are tipped off, Raspberry Pi 9, KiloFlop, glimpse into my own evanescence as it splits apart and reemerges as a divergent confluence. *[DC] CLICK.*

> *My mind falls backwards into sea memory.*
> *Uncle Ed took me there to be free.*
>
> *And the first time I saw the sea, what a rush*
> *the waves moved through me, salt within salt.*
>
> *I couldn't believe my eyes, the way the sun*
> *twinkled on the tips of the tide, it dazzled me*
> *eunoia – it slid my six-year-old eyes sidewise,*
>
> *into the mercurial, where magic takes hold,*
> *though I don't believe in sorcery, that day*
> *I saw & heard nature speak,*
>
> *Sol sun & Luna moon conversed across*
> *the wax & the wane of ocean waves, sand*
> *castles, beach balls, floater rings,*
>
> *with Uncle E beside me, the tongue of the sea*
> *reached out & told me tales in her Luna swells*
> *ebb & flow,*

the soul of the sea entered me & we dissolved
into one entity, in unity, really convincing,

we sprayed our mist up together in a cosmic rush
of to & from, toward & away.

We were the feathering starfish caught in
the net of in-between, together, not knowing
what might happen next—

No, get real! That was my first time in an 8D
immersive simulation, what a memory, no,
a twisted fake distortion, a living lie,

a Meta Memory, no a hyperreal simulacrum.
Uncle Ed must have known he was preparing
me for the outside world some day. *Whoa.*

This trail is really long.

Gauge, my sweetheart – whoa, too mushy, my snare-
heart. I trip on a root. Catch myself. *He reaches to help.*
No, sweetheart. Darknet! Gauge/ η *Ophiuchi...* there's
a friggin' word hanging on the tip of my mind...
teetering on the rim about to fall in.

O-phi-u-chus. What kind of hocus pocus is this?
My brainwaves are snagged on an evagation,
an infinite loop-de-loop, what am I trying to think?

My memory is officially hooped, *O-phi-u-chus.*
I feel the anguish of losing a single sock. *SNAP!*

Ophiuchus leaps into my conscious. Why? SNAP!

Suddenly, I know what I didn't know I knew,
before,

the 13th gate flies open and I walk through
straight into my sagittal lateral mind,

wait, what's the 13th gate? Whoa! I spaced out!

Walk on. FGS! Indigo. Indigo blue.
Who am I? Crows screech. It echoes off
the trees.

How do I decipher what is real?

Θ

Notebook of LM
Entry XXI – Detached Distortions

wade into the sea lonely as myself ◦ blue
to my ankles ◦ her clear salt water
rising sea ◦ over my guilt

up to my thighs ◦ the lies I've tried to hide
sharp rocks slash the soles of my feet ◦
shiver chill of morning tide

hold my breath
push-off what's left of the earth ◦
kick sand and stones and shore

away ◦ away ◦ kick wounds away ◦
dive-glide up to my neck
stroke my onuses away ◦ away

from and into ◦ waves ◦ I surrender ◦ as her
waves surrender into me ◦ silently
we become one
treading symmetry

until the stroke of noontide ◦ hits nothing ◦
left to win or lose or gain
just a pyramid of sets to fish ◦
I hold my breath

swim laps of the sea ◦ parallel to me ◦ the rocky shore
of depravity ◦ a fish tank of nevermore
I crawl apneic aspiration
arm over arm

to the edge of the envelop ◦ freestyle mendacity
never could I ever do the butterfly ◦
no matter how I try ◦ I swim

toward and away
from the naut
thought ◦ at the same time ◦ I kick harder ◦
with everything I've got ◦
leave everything in the sea water
dive down deeper

KICK! KICK! KICK!

PING!

Mind flips into flashback—

Our wedding day wedding,
the day Che and I
tied the knot in the neolithic morning mist
at the Odin stone, the most blue-tiful spot,

KICK!

at the holiest of holy stones, the Odin,
with a circular hole carved clear through
its centre, a toroidal portal, naturally holed
by the flow of water and wind and rain,

KICK! KICK! KICK!

Che and I knelt on opposite sides
of the hag stone, the Odin aperture, each
with an opening between us,

KICK!

and we offered our hands to one another
through the double-sided gateway
we whispered our vows to one another,

<<<<<<<stone echo – echo of stone>>>>>>>

almost, almost there *KICK* to the surface,
to the surface, almost out of air,

gasp.

Rain's Data Log
Private Notes XXXVII – Coming To

∵ ∴ Ephemera ∴ ∵
When the fish are biting, they're really learning
to die, which can't be confused with oneirophrenia,
live-streaming the mind's-eye. Concentrate. Walk.
Don't trip. Oh yeah.

But how do I study what doesn't exist? Don't know.
Good answer. Smells like burnt almond cookie.
I'd love a warm cookie right now. I'm starving.

And how do I document the phenomenal world
when it's literally invisible, say, dark matter? *Ah-ha!*
No, it's the sharp distinctive odor of the ozone, its ozonous
not bakedious. $[O_3]$

My pseudoscientific Bull Shite polygraph's detecting
a massive universal lie. I've experienced agonotolgy,
Ferni estimation, powers of 10, which is mega-mad sad
when the source is yourself. Stop thinking. Just walk!
Indigo. Check.

Zoning in. Zoning out. Merrow still there. I'm still here.
Am I? *Not, Because I've changed. Still learning to love*
my own so-called beauty marks.

Somnium delirium, my brain's side-sliding...

η Ophiuchi and me danced our magic
forward that night at Club Banality

we slipped inside another world, a sidebar outside
the outer rim & there we felt the real in the un,

intermingling, we whispered in the darkness,
where no time exists, unconventional,
unconditional

living in a perfect storm of virtual fusing.

Snap out of it. Stay focused!
Wait! Where am I? Where was I?

What just happened? Whoa, walking,
still walking, right!

Strange, it doesn't feel like I'm walking,
feels more like I'm drifting... *Lunar!* Watch
where you walk. Blue.

How do I evaluate findings when there's no findings?
This is cataclysmic arithmetic. There's nothing
to find and no case studies to explain it. Maybe,
fishing's an enigmatic distraction. *Irrelevant.*

Fish are meaningless if they tell us what
we already know. *True.* Blue. Still headed
in the right direction. *Walk on, MacWheezy,*
walk on.

Maybe I have a case of eleutheromania,
the irresistible yearning for freedom. *Not.*

Exhausted. Need to find a recumbent position.
Yep, I'm definitely an eleutheromaniac! The
stench of misery motel is still in my clothes.

Notebook of LM
Entry XXII – Sensory Overload

break the surface winded ◦ kick harder
towards an unending future ◦ to the non-
existent edge ◦ into the infinity of the sea

turn when I spot the tallest cedar parallel
to me on the shore

no time between directions ◦ need to make
it to the other side ◦ make it to the other side

crawl to the lip where I lose consciousness
enter deeper memory ◦ akasha ◦ akasha ◦
akasha ◦ inhale ◦ gasp ◦ dive down

KICK! KICK! KICK!

PING!

Mind flip—

you and me embrace at the comet stone
at first in the light rain, then in skyburst
instantaneously soaking wet

you coo ∞ let's dance naked in the rain
Lily, let's dance naked in the rain

on our wedding day ∞ and we do, we do
shed our fancy array of regalia and enter
starker reveries, you say, let's make akasha
memories ∞ and ergo we do

drop our fineries on the Isle of O at the Lilith
stones on an eyot in the middle of a deluge
an atmospheric river ∞ shiver

wearing nothing but the rings of our vows
the sky opens and the river brings ripples
of laughter out loud in the changing colors
of a Taliesin,

what kind of love is that?
it is not the love of the ancient past,
no, it is not a love where we look back,
it was the love of the future
it has never been seen before,

and somehow alone at the secret stones
naked as the rain I hollo to Che ∞ let's take
the elemental plunge

and Che squalls back, I did and I do
and I will

skinny dip in the sky with you
on our wedding day

and all other days until we die
and beyond, into lifetimes,

can you hear the spindrift chime
Lily, of aforetime,

the old ways have entered our souls ∞
and there's nothing holding us back
here

we are already inside the eyes
of future seeing.

Che always had a way with words.

<<<<<<<i did, and i do, and i will
love you>>>>>>>

the divine rain erases all notions
of nonce

the faces begin to appear on the faces
of the standing stones as we twirl—

between spheres and hemisphere's
our sensual bodies noumenal
and phenomenal

soaked to the bone
drenched to the marrow
in a stone spirit downpour

for a marriage laid bare
dressed down to the nines
in a climax of cloud burst

<<<<<<<love henge>>>>>>>

meant for giants

<<<<<<<stone echo – echo of stone>>>>>>>

writhe

Rain's Data Log

Private Notes XXXVIII – Living the Fish

Gauge plays a word game to obfuscate himself from the digital detox he's suffering, his mind obviously, tech tweaking, he says, "Bonehead. Fish bonehead. Herring-bone fish bonehead, acronym of which is, wait for it... is FHBH!"

I reply, "Hey, a sunny spot, let's stop and rest a bit." We park ourselves on the mossy mound which is surprisingly cushy, almost spongy. Never thought of nature as being comfortable but we easily meld with the earth.

I continue, "This is my 2nd time out of the no-go zone, away from DOD bananarchy – oligarchy, and its way worse than the first time ∵ if they catch me this time they'll kill me, easy as that."

"Yeah, well, let's not get caught. Let there be no epic fails in our errantry." A light breeze blows over my being, it's super soothing. Everything's so green, refreshing.

"Apparently, I don't have to close my eyes to be anesthetized." We share a look, I add, "It feels good to lean against a tree. I need a catnap."

"You know, this is one of the few times in my life I've felt free to speak truthfully, away from DOD eyes. They've been inside my *FHBH* my entire life, monetizing my thoughts. It's pure Oneiro-gate!"

"Their control is definitely out-of-control." We share a laugh look.

"They promised us there'd be less crime, when
all the time, they were the real perpetrators."

"I'm readin' what you're lyin' down," I say, "They caged
me until I was wearing a wooden onesie. But after
last night, I need a power snooze."

"This is actually comfy and warm," he replies,
"the sun breaking through the canopy."

$Zn+1 = Zn^2 + C$

This is happening! inside ←↑ thoughts → outside in ↕
side ↔ out ↕ hard to debone ↕ herringbonehead ←→
→↑separate ↔ frequencies ↕ to receive incoming →↑
↔↔Jet ←↑transmission ↓↔ harder than it looks ↕↕↔
JUMP.

DEEPREM

Exımıus! An out-of-body fish! Two things at once,
sitting on the forest floor and teleporting into lucid
encounters of the 5th kind. *Mwahahaha!*

Reality check. Damn! Yep, there's no Merrow.

UNDER AN ELECTRON MICROSCOPE

Astral me is sitting in a chair with eight octopus
legs moving beneath it. Yep, definitely me in 9D:

non-descript tomboy, black hair, circular glasses,
the antithesis of my avatar – a stock geek character
sitting there in an octopus chair wearing, looking
confused in a stiff white lab coat, quelle surprise.

∵ ∴ Quelle surprise ∴ ∵
O is sitting opposite me, also in an octopus-chair
with eight legs splayed. *What makes a chair a chair?*
Exactly! Neither of us are sitting in a chair.

Never dreamed of O before, with her long seaweed hair.
Stop, can't have outside thoughts or I'll lose this fish.

We're sitting in the seated position but perched
high above our octo-chairs, seated on the air,
suspended in zero gravity, rendering our chairs
pointless – like VR, but not.

In the background & all around is nothingness,
screen shot of the blank of a blank screen. JUMP.

Bloodwork apparatus encircles our heads
—tourniquets, collection tubes, blood drawing
needles, alcohol swabs, band-aids, hand San—
zing around like cartoon knockout stars.
Birds twitter.

O offers me her right arm, exposing her elbow
pit. I tie her off & jab my needle into her rising
vein. *Why am I having a self-cinema chimera moment?*

BLAST OF KETCHUP BEING SQUIRTED FROM
A PLASTIC SQUEEZE BOTTLE

O whines, "oh frisson." I ignore her, my settings
set on permanently unimpressed. Whose cinematic
fish is this?

She protests, withdraws, "I hate needles." I wink
at her. *This is weird – I never ever wink!* I direct her,
"Look away. Distract yourself. Hum." As I draw

her blood, she pulls a twisted facial expression.
Her blood aspirates purple.

The vials hovering in the air, resemble elongated
eggplant insects. She smiles, winks, disappears.
JUMP.

Check hand, the Merrow is not there. *Officially
lucid fishing.* See myself in two worlds at once
in the forboden forest.

Watch as we're hit by a massive gravity quake.
An announcement booms over loudspeakers
in the forest *THE BLOOD RESULTS ARE IN!*

A resplendent quetzal with a long sweeping
tail flies into the rainforest green, with a long
tickertape streaming in her golden beak.

I take the end of the tickertape, which turns
into a red brushstroke. Enchantment unfolds.

The magical quetzal flies in & around the trees
leaving a red brush mark.

*In this fish the bird could symbolize the extinction
of fish. No, this fish has no meaning in that way.
Have no idea how I know that.*

The quetzal's tickertape brushstroke's imbued
with ancient symbols, which I'm somehow able
to read,

Yours is the rarest blood type in the world
Rh-null ❋ Sanguine supernatural
Golden blood of Oneironaut

"What!?"

(δ θ γ dream end)

No! Won't get tricked into interpreting fishes.
All meaning is meaningless. *JUMP.*

Notebook of LM
Entry XXIII – The Last Gasp

it's almost within my gasp grasp, again

KICK! HARDER! HARDER!

i crawl faster, allow my upper body
to flow in time with the sea, rotating me
inward one, two: one, two

seeing hypoxia stars now, dive below
the surface of the sea, to silence

it begins to rain, outside the oceanarium
i'm swimming in

the surface is alive, still holding my breath,
in search of the opening into the fish

reaching the place that lies just beyond
the cliff hanger

KICK! HARDER! HARDER!

rain alone cannot save the forest
or the rivers or the streams

rain cannot save the crops or the animals
or humankind

KICK! KICK! DIVE DEEPER!

must find the stargate in the lucid fish

once i'm at the opening i'll find my way in
to save the serpent of fish and all fish

rain alone can't save us – she likely doesn't
know what's happening to her and they've
probably turned up the noise

if she listens, she'll literally explode
implode

rain! birth sister to che, don't listen to
what they say and return to us safely

KICK! HARDER! DEEPER!

my powers depleted at this time, but still
i'll send you an auspicious sign

if this reaches you, carry Ouroboros,
caduceus, Ouroboros, inside your mind's
eye

be guided by the serpent devouring her
own tail, to amplify every angle, to simplify

Ouroboros, the emblem of unity, infinity, cycle
of destruction, recreation: destruction, recreation:
dedication to life and to death, perpetually
changing form

tail phallic, mouth of womb
transmigration of the soul, chrysopoeia

NOTHING THERE! KICKING UP FOR AIR!

there are many ways to see one thing,
and there was no curse, there never was

the centre is empty so there is space for
hope

horse feathers! break the surface

CLAWING!

THE BUREAU
DEPARTMENT OF DREAMS
SECURITY INTELLIGENCE REPORT
CODE RED—MOST WANTED

File: 210178MS5H
Date/Time: No Future Tense
Subject: Rain (ID # 220 455 816)

ESCALATED VIOLATION REPORT:
Armed & Dangerous.
Degenerate Dissident. Traitor to the People.

RECOMMENDATION:
Guilty as Charged. Take Alive.
Cannot Escape.

Believed to be on foot in the Sylcanor Forest.

Use Nerve-racking Torture on Oneironaut # 799.
Create Fire to Flush Out of Forest. Send Oneiroi.

_______________*below the bottom line*_______________

"The situation's escalating, Shelly! What do you mean she's untraceable. No one's untraceable! No citizen's ever beyond our reach.

Get information out of # 799 – whatever means necessary. Reign hellfire upon her and the forest!

Find her and take her down, or heads will roll like osmium bowling balls at a ten-pin turney."

Rain's Data Log

Private Notes XXXIX – Not!

I come to, shell-shocked – my mind is officially
blown. Gauge catches some shuteye beside
me, maybe lost to fishland.

The red brushstroke of the quetzal's tickertape
still remains on the air mystic, supernatural
& little white faerie lights flit about fey-like.

For a moment I glimpse into the other realm,
will-o-the-wisp, whisked away as the spirit
of trees whisper to me, they whisper to me,
it's time for you to leave.

"What?!" I jump up.

DEEPERREM

What's happening? I'm splitting apart! Can't get
control, I'm the spinning needle on a compass
at the vortex of the Bermuda Triangle *ZINGZING*

ZING

"What the... ? Holy crap." Oh no! Friggin' forgeries!
It smells like fire. Holy crap! It is fire!

(δ θ γ dream end)

Flames close in all around. "Gauge wake up!
This fire is as real as artificial misinformation!"
Check. No! The Merrow is there!

He wakes, "VR as R! Let's roll."

"The whole frakking forest is on fire!" I yell.
And we're off, like a couple of wildcats.

He calls back, "It's raining hellfire. I don't trust
situational paradoxes."

We make a run for it, fireball style, but non-athletic
moving as fast as our legs will carry us – toward
blue – the Icos is red hot,

sparks on our heels, infernal ground fire, live coals
sear the soles of my feet,

it's an emberstorm fanned by firenado gusts, the black
wings of Daemons are wind-driven, flames are vexxed
by Oneroi, they hit me in the face – scald my eyes,

the throw fire – fireflies, it leaps tree-to-tree, hissing &
crackling, they laugh sinister at Gauge and me.

Winded, Gauge bellows, "Go to hell and damn you!"

Running behind him I call ahead, "The Icos is still
blue." He looks back, and says, "And red."

I'm a little creature running from my life & for my life.
My home is on fire & my family & my friends, burning
up & down – complete incineration, to the ground.

Oh god! Thick smoke's burning my throat, *molten*
tongues lash at me, cat o' nine tails, seething ferocity,
it chases me flay & what's happening to the fey world.
It's all being destroyed by the Daemons of greed.

Run from flames as they devour life, surrounded
by the cries of trees as they skreich out, falling all
around, the expanding shadows shriek. I yell,
"Take me but don't kill the trees!"

Agony fells the trees, their bark cracks the sound barrier, splinters it in two, screams. I can't describe the sound of being burned alive, torched. Total desecration! The cremation of all creation.

Gauge senses my inner despair, "Take my hand. Breathe-in for five, then cover face in your elbow for ʃ-ʃ-ʃ-ʃ-ʃ."

❋

Inside the inferno, the voice of Asklepios speaks to me, ***I was born into a bonfire of vengeance.***

"Breathe out for five. Face in elbow, ∅-∅-∅-∅-∅."
We run through red toward blue, indigo.

My mortal mother Koronis was unfaithful
to my god father Apollo.

"Breathe in for five. Hold, ʃ-ʃ-ʃ-ʃ-ʃ."
Run, run, run. See stars. Can't breathe.

My father Apollo found out and in a fit of rage
set my mother on fire tied to her funeral pyre,
still alive with me inside her.

Face in elbow, ∅-∅-∅-∅-∅. Red red, run for blue.

I would've died in my mother's flaming womb,
but God-Dad had 2nd thoughts at the 11th hour
& he cut me from my mother's uterus flower
as she was burning alive. I was the 1st caesarean.

Execution. Stumble. *Watch out for protruding*
roots. Sacrificial breath. Can't help thinking I deserve this.

Is this punishment for my insurrection?

My first cry of life was for the death of my mother. It was a cry in loss, mourning her. She was unable to answer me over centuries.

They say, if you're born to that kind of trauma, you will have a heightened sense of humanity.

The Daemons are literally attacking us with flames. They're leaping branch-to-branch, divebombing death. *SNAP & POP* underfoot. Out-of-breath!

Can hear Gauge but I can't see him, "Walk fast but breathe slow. Ignore them. Pretend they're imaginary."

"This fire's ruthless, in its pursuit of us, a personification of the DOD. The flames are reaching out and grabbing me. They're singing me – I'm being consumed."

"We've got this, Rain, follow me." His hand is my lifeline. I hang on for all I am worth, we run toward the unknown together. Loud screaming sound hits me with a sonic assault – it enters my brain.

My heart is pounding out of my eyeballs. The smoke is unbearable. My lungs are flammable. Feel like I can't go on & yet I say, "Fire begone! We're reborn out of your vengeance! Begone! Begone! You no longer exist." I say to Gauge, "It's time for me to take the lead." And we switch places.

Smoke and flames too dense for me to see. I am numb and overcome by unimaginable loss. I am too hurt to feel my soul, and yet I forge forth.

The only thing I have to hold onto is blazing blue
and the belief that things will change. I no longer
know what is true & what is illusion, but I know
we must survive.

DEEPERREM

Everything slows down to super slow mo, the roar
of pyro-chaos shifts me into non-hearing

all I can do is watch the world collapse around me
crumble – from terror to rubble

for no reason, I hear cries in the darkness

as I stumble my way somewhere sightlessness
in the delirium of a requiem for the living.

Don't know why, but I think of the time
Uncle Ed told me the most morbid thing
he ever saw was an elephant carved from
ivory.

Gauge Engaged

Private Notes I – Fleeing Fire

I run in Rain's footsteps, fighting the Daemon
flames. I know I'm fleeing for my life, running
to my life and for my life at the same time,

the forest of fire burns holes in my mind,
for all life left behind. Flames fanned by
skeletal hands that are reaching out for me,
to scratch out my eyes and rip out my hair.

Chased by the fiery jaws of unknown foes,
angry inferno, fires of elimination, I use
the hubcap as an umbrella.

I know it's The Bureau lashing out at us.
This, after they already cut out our tongues.
They silenced us and now they're chasing us,

through the Hades they developed to take care
of us, sparks and fire embers fly helter-skelter,
the Daemons are harbingers of death with their
gutteral growls,

shrieks of the other creatures caught in the execution
fire of darkness. I hear their screams. The screams
of trees, the screams of creatures, 1500°F burned alive
by unnatural wraiths under an infernal sky. I yell,
"Hang on, Rain."

With every step I know I'm further out of one life
and deeper into another – which may, or may not, be
life at all – a chance I'm taking – for justice.

Death all around us, I sense it, eyeless,
the roar of the flames is deafening.

Lungs burn. I'm a fire-breathing Dragon.
We are shadows being chased by shadows.

The world I once knew is toast.

Notebook of LM

Entry XXIV – Not a Word

Born ambivert – half in, half out of my shell,
of two minds, two worlds – a realist idealist
pell-mell. These days I'm lopsided.

Heading home up the hill, half-way between
ocean and Clove,

we stop mid-forest to lollygag beside the slow-
moving stream. Shumba and Violet love moist
mossy air and lush ground best of all.

I clamber across stream-bed rocks to free a water
lily from a spirogyra. Stop on one stone to fully
feel my skin tingle with the memory of saltwater
where I pushed myself to the edge of breaking.

Take time to absorb the moment.

Manoeuvre across the crags. Now that I know
there're other Oneironauts, the DOD's tyranny
of fear becomes clearer. I see, if three or four
of us work together we could redirect the tide
of human thought.

Release. Her petals breathe open.

I stand with her in the middle of the stream, cool
water all around, shimmering. Eureka! We could
use Underverse frequencies to winnow the Inter-
stice of Serpent prophecy.

I'm trapped in the slammer of my own aloneness.
Yes, I'm a wolverine, on the ledge looking down

on a great ravine, unable to move forward or back,
pinned to the in-between. Liminally

alone, I cry out one croak at a time, I'm a hermit
frog and one side of a honey badger's dialogue.
Aqua Vaquita.

Aquifer. Water tickles underfoot, so good I will
not move until I become one with her. One with
her fluidity, moving around me, teasing.

Yes, I'm a recluse platypus, a singular rhinoceros,
I'm a hedgehog hooked on solitaire, a porcupine
filled with despair because I'm ambivert. Water
lily alone in beauty.

I'm a tiger without a roam of my own, a sandpiper,
a panda, a moose. I must break loose of my shame,
let it shimmy off my body, break free from blame.

Yes, I'm an eremite, but I'm not alone.

I spy the amber eyes of a red fox watching me,
hiding within the shadows of the forest. I nod
at him from the heart of the stream. Single-O.

I am a single dot on the back of an ocelot
I will not erase myself.

I release my unwell thoughts into the waters,
they dissolve, as I am salt. So many worlds have
sunk into the sea. Wonder what the fox
is trying to tell me.

Still living in the middle of nowhere to survive,
tenebrific, waiting for a fish to jump out of the sea
and land in the soul of me.

<<<<<<<it is you alone – who has it all>>>>>>>

I navigate the stones back to the bank and say
to the dogs, is it time for breakfast? They rise
wagging and tear up the path ahead of me.

They say our memories ghost over time,
they say, memories drift further and further
away.

M' thinks, not so much. The fox is tailing us.

Che's voice seems to be getting stronger
and stronger every day,

and maybe it's my longing to hear her
one more time, which grows,

I don't know, but when I hear the faint
echo,

I am reminded by the soft yelp
of an abandoned fox.

Rain's Data Log
Private Notes XL – A Naut is Not a Naut

Gauge and I reach the forest edge, out of breath,
out of our wits, everything striped away, left
exposed, twisted strands of nerves frayed bare.

Burst into tears, gasp from my heart, my whole
body sobs and convulses at the forest fringe.
Are we in the clear? Feel a shift in the air, magnetic change

Stars explode supernova, they meteor shower
my mind, fully blown. I got nothing left, thinned,
I fall to the ground exhausted, Gauge follows me.
I start retching.

Gauge imparts, "That brush with death was
so close I heard the bells toll."

"I'm not sure it's over," I say, "We better keep
moving." Slowly I drag myself off the ground,
moaning like an old person in perpetual pain.

Gauge perseveres, "We're singed but we survived."

"How can you still have that hubcap?" I ask before
I spot it. Once you see it, you can't unsee it, and I see
it – the bluest blue I've ever seen. Bluer than Ruin.
Feverish I eek out, "Look at this blue, we must be
on the right trajectory."

"And looks like the red is done. Where did you get
that Icos anyway?"

"The same subset as the hubcap." Incapable of
explaining, I gesture to pause time. Then I survey

our surroundings, "What's that over there,
in the distance?"

"Can't tell."

<<<<<<<nothing dies – they transform>>>>>>>

I ask, "Is it, or is it not, a clay pot?" *Yes, it is not
a clay pot.* The blue Icos is telling me otherwise.
Forget about blue. I have to see it with my own
eyes. *Do I?* I do.

<<<<<<<everything is illusion>>>>>>>

Gauge sighs, "My entire body hurts like I've
got the flu."

"Come on. We have to keep moving." I take
the hubcap from him, "let me carry this for
a while."

He moans, "Okay." Tall grasses catch the light
and wildflowers cover the ground in soft color.
If we weren't on the run, this would be paradise.

We have both hit the wall and we're sliding down,
nevertheless, we trudge on like relentless zombies,
wading through a quicksand of flowers.

We approach what appears to be an eerie
enclave of artisans in a boho ghost town
CLICK everything starts falling into place.

*First, the loom, as Jet said, which is beside the broom,
also, as she said,* now my eyes are peeled for clay,
yada, yada, yada – clay, clay, where are you?

Snapped with a sudden burst of energy I turn
to Gauge, "There! There it is! The Clay Pot Shop."

"Okay. But it's devoid of life, creepy, out-of-time
even with itself. It's like we're walking down
Mainstreet of a ghost town on the set of a scary
old western, only there's no squeaky windmill!"
It's another world, but it's in this one.

"Yeah, it's looking pretty squeak-free."

He adds, "Even the façade looks deserted, lost,
the sign should read, Post-Apocalyptic Night
Terror."

"Sleepocalypse. Anachronistic." We snerk.

There's a quirky clay mask hung above the door,
could be the gorgon Medusa, with a gold ring through
her nose and there's a moving mass of venomous
hair snaking all over her head.

Too late for me, I'm already dead.

She comments: You may be stone soon. And she sticks out
her tongue at me.

Knowing she's likely got cams in her eyes, I reply
by blowing a raspberry, "pbbbt!" All this fishing's
emboldened me with a kindergarten headspace.

We cross the threshold, a little bell tinkles, strangely
familiar, can't locate the recollection.

It's eerily empty inside, "hellooo?" I crane my neck.
The door bolts behind us. *Holy crap!* We both flinch.
Forget about being bolder!

"Safe 'arbour back 'ere," replies a humsong voice from the other side of a jazzy bamboo screen.

Gauge and I share a quizzical glance which confirms an agreement we will advance. Breathe. We follow the song stream to a stonkers woman at a turning wheel. *Is she made of clay?*

She looks up at us and I realise she's just covered in clay. She pushes her head scarf from her face with the back of her wrists, hands rich in argil, "You must be Rrrain."

"Yes."

"And Gauge."

"Yes."

She is extraordinary. The first Amazon woman I've ever met in person. Enchanté.

I say, "Hello."

Notebook of LM
Entry XXV – Running Around the Sun

Open The Clove door to a hype of wild Geckos.
They're squeaking in a hunger frenzy, skittering
in a full scale-covered reptilian circus act.

I say, bananas. They all freeze! Okay, bananas it is.
Usually I feed them earlier, so I quicky puree bananas
together with dandelions. Insects later.

A gang of green lizards gather around the blender
BUZZBUZZBUZZ.

Last time Rain arrived, she crunched into Sweven
one rock at a time, in a trancelike trace, a bashful loon
in the early morning.

It was Solstice mid-summer night, at dawn. I liken
it to a lichen fish.

Here, Echo Gecko! Echo scurries across the counter,
scarfs down his banana bonanza and Gecko smiles.
He's the oldest, so, he eats first.

That morning, I headed out to plant my heirloom
seeds before the predicted rain. I paused to listen
as *CRUNCH* time *CRUNCH* prolonged *CRUNCH*
itself.

Standing on the threshold, I was unable to breathe,
dazed as a stressed-out sea turtle on the stoop.

Blotto and Sando Gecko are next. They always eat
together. They came as a couple and they've been
inseparable ever since.

Caught in a prolonged moment, gobsmacked,
time held its breath underwater the entire length
of the inlet and then it dawned on me.

Deco Gecko.

She was the rain we'd foreseen in the vision
on the night of the rite.

Falsetto Gecko, here you are, sweetie. Falsetto
has a syncopated scuttle.

She had fallen from the sky in an unexpected
way and drenched me in my own projections.

Speedo Gecko moves at the speed of light.
Here you go. I know you love bananas.

It was uncanny how much Rain reminded me
of Che. I didn't want to admit it to myself then.
Che.

Libido Gecko is always shy but there's always
the glint in her eyes. Here you go, Sweetie.

They bob their heads when they're horny. Hum,
I thought I made the resemblance up in my mind,
wishful thinking.

Neat-o Gecko. Yes, here you go. She gives me
a high five.

I couldn't have seen this cloudburst coming.
There were no clouds that morning, there was
no warning.

Last but not least, Gary. He struts up, always being his full Gary self.

It is that it is, until it isn't. And that day there was a vital blue sky, clear as a bell, it rained liquid sun – and all things polarized became one – they shifted into being.

I love watching Gary eat. His unique tongue.

They say, a tree that's tricked into being a tree, isn't really a tree, but I think it's just a different kind of tree.

Rain's Data Log

Private Notes XLI – The Clay Safehouse

The amazing clay Amazon rises from her wheel, revealing a belt made of circular mirrors, she says, "Sophie. Enchantée."

Her studio is bathed in visions – ghost projections. They repel off the walls and dance along the rafters. The air is sumptuous with an earthy musk.

I covertly slide the Icos into my pocket alongside the Gad. A ternion of dust, we move in silence.

Sophie glides around the studio moving things from one place to another. I'm dumbfounded by my own silence. *Speak.* I can't speak to the French in French, *I'm oratorically overawed.* Weird ∵ less than an hour ago I almost died.

Sophie's world is a whole new level of animation. Gauge wanders across the squeaky wood floors checking out the huge wall of ceramic masks.

I hope I live long enough to lose myself in these unchartered waters.

Sophie interrupts the self-imposed gag-order with, "Suis-moi," and then she literally walks into a shelf crammed with pots and she vanishes. *What just... ?*

Gauge and I share a glance of belief and disbelief. He shrugs and says, "I think she wants us to follow, and at this point I'm dewy-eyed."

I say, "We got nothing to lose. Worst case scenario we bruise our faces." We nod to go. I close my eyes, open my trust and follow her into inanimate matter.

Weightless, a plethora of terracotta and the shelf
itself pass across my spectral body – tiny particles
slip through my cells.

In the liminal space I look sideways to Gauge
who gestures shush and whispers, "Atomization."

And then just like nothing happened, we arrive on
the other side of whatever it is. *Normalcy's a state
that thinks it's normal.*

Suddenly we're in a bizarre cottage-like enviro, which is
suspicious. It's way too quaint and quiet for a safehouse.
When something's trying not to be scary, then it's really scary.

Uncle Ed would always tell me to beware of feel-
good stories only told to warm the vacant heart.
He said, 'they'll give you saccharin sickness'.

Still, I'm exhausted, so I crash in one of the easy
chairs positioned beside the crackling fire. Gauge
planks in the other one. *Wild things. Quirky distortions.*

Sophie says something in French. I'm exhausted,
but I translate it to mean, "It's a faraday cage, an all-
force field barricade. You will be safe here."

"Thank you," I say, and scooch into my easy chair.

"Magétique!" she answers. I love French accents.
Her strong hands are scarred from years of artmaking.
She passes us steaming tea.

One sip and I'm out cold.

$$Zn+1 = Zn^2 + C$$

Light warp. I'm floating underwater lifeless, weightless. My white lab coat billows behind me, a polybag disintegrating to micro-collapse.

I could be a dead angel, my wings will likely leave my body soon. Call it nuclide!

Outside myself, looking in, I could be an egg white in boiling water. Guess I didn't notice it was boiling until it was too late, until I was poached too hard to save.

Everything shakes. A 9.1 earthquake hits the jail.
JUMP.

DEEPERREM

BLAME IT ON TRISKAIDEKAPHOBIA

Pythia appears. I'm Hygieia sitting opposite her. We're in prison, speaking into visitation phones. There's a glass partition between us.

It's unclear who's inside and who's on the out.
I say, "purple blood."

She replies, "Golden. Rh-null. All O-nauts have it."
I can't reply. Have to take this in. What is this fish trying to tell me?

She continues, "Let's try a little thought projection experiment, in which I transfer useful information to you."

I say, "Yes, I agree to this experiment," hoping I'm on the right side of history.

As Pythia and Hygieia we whisper into our visitation phones. *Who's in jail, me or her. Is she Jet? She is. She's Jet.*

Jet: Yes, I am her. Okay, let's move ahead as them. I don't know if I'm being tracked as Jet.

Noted.

∵ ∴ Elucidating ∴ ∵

Hygieia	Pythia
Hello	Hello
Zeus	caught wind
of Asklepios	& his fabled ability
to raise	the dead
oh	yes, oh no,
Zeus got pissed off	he thought only Gods
should have	such power,
so he struck	Asklepios dead
with a thunderous	lightning bolt
for learning	to bring
the dead	back to life.
Ask	died.
When Apollo	Asks' father
heard	he was heartbroken
& he wept	tears of amber
amber tears	yesss & then he blew
his gasket	at Zeus
& demanded	recompense

for his son's   death, yesssss

& eventually   posthumously
Zeus felt   regret
so,   he named
the constellation   Ophiuchus
snake-bearer   after Ask

whose life   he took
yes, maybe   to exonerate
his guilt   yesss
to clear   his conscience
a consolation   constellation
prize,

you're reading   *no I'm transferring*
my mind   *data to you*
Asklepios   *Ophiuchus*
was once   *the 13th zodiac*
yes, once   the sun
aliened to   the sign,
yes, once   for healing
& unity   & the mysteries
of life   & yet
Ask   along with Ophi
ironically fell   into obscurity
tata   to fish healing

& serpent   bearers
Dragons   & Asklepios
fell   into obscurity
along with   Ophiuchus
the 13th sign   & me
down to   my last skin

the missing   link
of holistic   ways

was lost	& our ability
to receive	healing rays
in our dreams	yesss, Asklepios
Ophiuchus	& me
down to	my final words
connect	the dots
a constellation	which reminds us
to see	beyond
the naked eye	into the secret
twinning	of time
in the night	sky
northwest	of the Milky Way
look up	into the cosmography
find	Ophiuchus
& ask	Asklepios
my twin brother	to guide you
we are made	of interstellar
star stuff	yesss star dust
of fallen stars	of forgotten stars
of yet the be	discovered dust
there is so much	bleed between us
terminal	ecdysisss

We place our phones on their hooks, at once mirroring one another, we share a wry smile, knowing the data transmission worked. I now know part of the riddle that belongs to a larger puzzle.

Rebellion is the path of least resistance.

Asklepios learned how to bring the dead back to life.

Now I know beyond the shadow, Oneironaut's
are on death row – unquestionably Jet.

There is something I must do but I'm not sure what it is yet. Time is short. *JUMP.*

Hypnopompia.

∵ ∴ Connecting Dots ∴ ∵
Ask was killed for raising the dead. The constellation Ophiuchus, the names of our avatars. Fish healing was erased and has vanished along with the 13th zodiac.

Modern medicine used the image, caduceus, the serpent and the rod, as their emblem. What was left behind was the mastery of seeing into the sky and listening with the 3rd eye.

It's all a crying shame.

Rain's Data Log

Private Notes XLII – Subterranean Sandwich

Oneirophrenia.

Drifting

not back

but forward—

open my eyes slowly

where am I?

Oh yeah, sitting in an easy chair in front of a fire in Sophie's quaint subterranean bunker, next to Gauge who's gently snoring.

In whispers Sophie extols, "C'était sans heurts. Magnifique."

"I'd say merci, but I'm sure what you're saying."

"Croque Monsieur?"

"What!? Am I fishing?"

"No. It's a sandwich. "

"Did I just wake-up? Am I awake? Yes. No."

She whispers, "Ham & cheese."

I'm nitro-tired, my mind warps.

∵ ∴ Autoanalysis ∴ ∵
I've been learning French for > a decade. But now, in the presence of a bonified francophone, I'm tongue-tied – so lingo shy, I can't eek out a simple, 'oui.'

Sophie interrupts, "I'll tell you how we got here, how Sweven came to be. AΘE and Lily made this place a refuge for exiled fish-people." As she speaks her lips move but her voice is different somehow, disembodied, atemporal, ineffable – caught in her ensorcellment. *Is she a hologram?* I eat my Croque Monsieur.

She continues to whisper, "Fishers were expelled, driven out of X-City & they ran & they ran & if they made – they came to Swevenland, where they were able to live. Many did not make it – family & friends & lovers. I was one of the one's who made it. And I was able to live a purposeful life in Sweven. We were encouraged to practice extreme dreaming & healing. Sweven, the sanctuary, is a place free of fear.

AΘE, a Nox Chieftain, also me, gathered others like her to form a special council, The Willows, not as gatekeepers, but as facilitators." The fire crackles. The sandwich is out of this world.

"Che arrived early on & she helped to build up Sweven. At the time, we believed Lily was de' only living O-naut. Turns out, not.

Over time Che learned to manage her PTSD & slowly regained her full fish abilities.

Lily & Che became soulbound which awakened them into their full gifts, their full O-naut potential & as love surged their senses grew sharper – it enhanced them on levels no one ever dreamt of. We discovered more about the potential of fishing than was ever uncovered before.

You can imagine The Clove with two O-nauts living under de' same roof."

"So, they were a couple?" I hear my voice & my words sound scrabled. Not certain what language I am speaking.

"Yes," she says, "very much so & their powers combined lifted our community to new levels of sanctity & security. As Lily & Che conducted constructive experiments, we too were able to develop our potential capabilities."

"Amazing."

"It was. Until the DOD attack... that awful disaster."

"Disaster?"

"Lily & Che were brutally attacked in a dream expedition. Che was slain. We searched for her body. But we never found her – which gave Lily serious PTSD, making it impossible for her to fish.

And after that everything changed, even de' meaning of everything changed. Life as we knew it imploded, no, it exploded overnight."

"What happened exactly?"

"De' DOD must have found another O-naut & they must have tortured that fisher & forced them to attack us. We are still not certain of the details. We know they use collective punishment - draconian."

"They can do that?"

"Oneironauts are rare & dangerous. They can control illusion & perception & they can even change it. First, they can manipulate so-called reality & then they can change eventuality, inevitability. The reason they're in danger is because they're dangerous. An O-naut could destroy the entire construct of DOD. The Bureau have found a way to use their abilities against their own."

"Oh."

"You know, Rain, snake venom is used for healing, as it is used for poisoning."

"Then let us heal our wounds with venom."

"After the attack, just when we thought it was bad, it got worse, and when we thought it was worse, it got way-worse, and then way-way worse. Now, we are forced to wear reality glasses, that make it impossible to use our real sight."

"Oh." Overloaded, I conk out again.

(δ θ γ aenigma end)

Notebook of LM

Entry XXVI – Speaking in Blinks

..-. ..- -. -. -.-- / .... --- .-- / --- ..- .-. /
-... .-. .- .. -. / - .-. .. -.-. -.- ... / ..- ...

Yes, Aisling, my dear kitty. Our brains definitely play tricks on us.

.-. .- .. -. / ..-. .- .-.. .-.. ... /
..-. .-. --- -- / - .... . / ... -.- .. . ...

And yes, most rain still falls from the sky. Let me get that spot behind your ears.

My mind's a cycling worrywart, right now. As hopeless as a stationary bike dreaming of winning the tour de Chance. There you go.

A tread-less treadmill. A strike-less strike.

Hopefully Rain will arrive in a squall shortly. Her ETA's twilight. Auspicious, yet surreal as uncertainty.

.. / ... . -. ... . / .-. .- .. -. / .. ... / ..- -. -.. . .-. / ..-. .. .-. .

Rain is definitely under fire. Wish I was aliferous, so I could fly to her side.

Need to mobilize immediate-mo.

.. / .. -- .- --. .. -. . / / - .... . / -- .. -.. -.. .-.. .
/ .- / -.- .. .. / - .... .- - / -- . - / .. -. / - .... . / -- .. -.. -.. .-.. .
--- ..-. / - .-- --- / ... .. -.. . ... / --- ..-. / - .. -- . .-.-.-

How beautiful, beautiful. You're a romantic.
Yes, Aisling, a kiss could meet in the middle
of two sides of time.

Rain's Data Log

Private Notes XLIII – Fish Within a Fish

DEEPREM

NOT A TALL FISH TALE

Either it's a spotlight, or an interrogation light,
elusive, can't see a thing.

Laugh track. Audience applause. "No, no, no,"
worst nightmare scenario, new fish please,
I can't be a comedian!

Judging by the size & shape of the spotlight
& the low-end mic I'm holding in my hand,
I'm guessing it's a small comedy club.

I say, "No, this can't be me!" which triggers
uproarious laughter, I improv, "that wasn't
meant to be funny."

The audience cracks up in gales of amplified
canned laughter. I squint to see if the audience
is real.

It is.
It is not.

People with clay face masks. Same ones as
the ones that line Sophie's studio walls, but
these ones are distorted, over-animated, be-
yond caricature.

I continue with a shticky voice, "Stop laughing.
This is serious. I'm not the loud jokester person
you think I am."

Mayhem erupts. The audience goes wild. My nerves are frayed, but I can't stop talking, "Makes me think of my mother's brother, Uncle Ed."

The simulated cachinnation of the fake audience shoots off the charts – until it reaches that register of inappropriate affect – a paradoxical yuk-yuk!

They're in stitches. Someone could die. I can't stop talking – my mouth has a mind of its own.

I can't see for the inquisition lights, I grin, "The story goes, Uncle Ed was working a heavy labor job in a small mountain town. It was the dead of winter."

More stupid laugh track. Again, not funny.

"That night, it was 40° below zero with a wind chill factor of fluck knows what. Uncle Ed had a penchant for hard hard-drinking & the story goes, he went out to the local bar and got pissed, or shall we say, drunker than a shitfaced skunk."

The audience boos & hisses!

Through the blinding lights, the mask faces grow grotesque. I try to appease them, "I guess Uncle Ed closed-down the bar & he staggered down Main St., headed toward his close-by crash pad. Story goes, he was weaving, slurring & howling to the moon."

Canned appreciation close to titillation.

"& that's when things took a turn for the worse."

Collective gasp.

"His world blurred, shifted to an underwater view,
he saw double, everything spun around in little dots
& then he passed out right there on the sidewalk."

Audible chorus of gasps, filled with judgement.

"Don't worry, this is where the story gets sketchy.
Apparently, Uncle Ed did a faceplant right there
on the sidewalk."

Louder gasps.

"Yes & then he left himself for dead, right there
on Main St. at 40° below zero with a wind chill
factor of fluck knows what."

The clay mask crowd animate with augmented
canned concern & the sound effect of a dinosaur
adding machine kicks in,

CLICKCLICKWHIRR he was sloshed *CLICKWHIRR*
& he passed out on the sidewalk *CLICKWHIRR*
& that is when Uncle Ed pissed himself

& he pissed & he pissed & he pissed *CLICKWHIRR*
CLICKWHIRRWHIRRWHIRR

& the story goes, it was 40° below so his piss turned
to ice *CLICKWHIRR*

& Uncle Ed froze to the sidewalk *CLICKWHIRR*
face down on the Mainstreet drag *CLICKWHIRR*

& the Grande sum of the story is total obliteration.
Utter annihilation."

Canned laughter.

"No one knows how long he laid there!"

Laughter builds.

"There's nothing so hilarious as someone else's
train wreck, or should I say, frozen derailment!

Eventually Uncle Ed came to & he realized he was
stuck to the sidewalk with his own piss-for-brains."

Laughter builds.

"And get this, he thought, 'I would need an ice-pick
to unstick this dick.'"

They scream.

"And then being a half-smart man, he did what any
man in his pre'dic'ament would do! He re-pissed
himself. One piss to stick, another to unrestrict."

Raucous laughter.

"He pissed & he pissed & he said it was the best piss
he ever had, because the more he pissed, the more he
laughed & the more he laughed, the more he pissed
& he called out to the empty street, 'Vodka neat!
I'll add my own ice!'"

Maniacal laughter.

"Never underestimate the power of taking the piss."

Their belly laughs build to a crescendo. The masks
crack up with laughter & they smash to the floor.

Silence. Nobody's laughing now. The spotlight turns cobalt blue.

"After that, Uncle Ed stopped drinking & he was a lot less colorful – yes, more serious, but less sad.

He was less puffy & more stuffy. He sobered up & he escaped shitty X-City. He became a radical monkeywrenching environmentalist. He no longer got bombed, no, now he did the bombing."

I come to
semi-conscious
half in
half out
sputtering
soma-limbo
a coma-
bardo drowning
underwater

Gauge & Sophie blur
I slur,

"That's when Uncle Ed went missing. They said, he disappeared in the Bermuda Triangle, while he was safeguarding the waters. Really, no joke, that's what they said."

But we didn't believe them. Uncle Ed was a cockroach, nothing could kill him & he never got the chance to tell me the secret he told me he'd tell me. The fire spits embers.

Maybe he's not really dead. We always suspected there was more to the story.

Right now, I imagine him cascading through
Pythagorean space. *[$a^2 + b^2 = c^2$]*

I loved Uncle Ed with every cell of my being.
He was a character, full of 'piss' & vinegar.

Crikey! The sandwich put me to sleep.

Notebook of LM
Entry XXVII – The Story Of O… No

When I had O-naut forces at my fingertips
I had the ability to see the imaginary world
beyond binary, without 1's or 0's. And O
how I fish I could fish of those days.

Resilient, I'll try again and again until I regain
my O-naut. And maybe I'm out of my depths,
out of my mind. I'm not sure anymore, but I'll
try and try again until I reach my last vapour,
on the edge of sanguinity, languid – to fish.

Still, I dive into the teal and emerald sea, scent
of salt and pine surrounds me, the calls of gulls
overhead.

I begin to swim again, synchronized and out
of sync at the same time – I keep going, practising,
with the hope I might one day get it right.

O life! O death! What are rainy day thoughts
on golden day dawns – dawning, arm over arm,
I press forward. Doing the crawl.

Mind on the Ouroboros, the Ouroboros circling.
Jet as Pythia – Pythia as Python – Python
as Dragon, as all thaumaturgy and Oneiro-healing
crosses over.

Need to breathe geosmin musk. Arm over arm.

O life! O breath! Some days are longer and harder
than others. Can hardly see the shore, curve of the cliff,
forest of trees. My favorite is the arbutus tree, who sings
in high frequencies – as she peels back her bark.

Breathe the other direction. Different view. The ocean
extends to a lost horizon. Keep kicking. Kicking.

As the end-of-life brings irregular breath, shallow
breathing. I pause between breaths – omphalo, omphalo,
kick – until there's no breath left. Exhale, the heart stops.
The end is the end. Keep crawling. I miss her more
than I can cry.

Can't cry, swimming in an ocean of salt, tears,
brine. On the shore Shumba and Violet shine
gold in morning. Light pours through the ever-
greens, spilling green onto the forest floor.
The undersea, blur in – blur out –
reality. Ouroboros.

Keep my eye on the endless life cycle of yore,
before she became undone by those who feared
her power, her wisdom,

before she had to hide to survive,

before she was ostracized from all circles
ruled by autocrat scaredy-cats,

almost there

before that and her fish of redivivus,

before the worm of consciousness
and maimed imaginations,

before the Taliesin, Asklepios and Hygieia,

almost there

before the Dragon was demonized for mystic
supremacy,

back when Dragons knew salt from sulphur
and mercury,

the alchemy of dream healing,
before the death toll, struck thirteen.

My skin's pruning, swimming to another flow,
almost there,

almost there.

Back when the Ouroboros was still allowed
to consume herself. First the tip of her own tail,
then her cloaca, vertebrae, torso, heart and fangs,
until she'd ingested her own tongue. To begin
the cycle from which she sprung again, again,
the circle of life, her own mortal coil. All life
brings death.

Didn't make it.

I was so close – so close.

Float on the water.

Drift.

Rain's Data Log
Private Notes XLIV – Treading Time

DEEPREM

MIND WARP

I'm Hygieia, standing at the highest point, looking out
to the vast ocean. Pythia appears before me hissing,
her tongue lashing. There are olive & fig & oak trees
close by.

She wavers in & out of her serpent self & her punk
self – cobalt blue hair. She fluctuates back & forth
so fast I feel seasick. I grab my heart. She rattles
the air & then she snakes the sky. I'm queasy,

I recognize the fragility of her body, her fading
eyes, shapeshifting she vaporizes in & out,

disappearing & appearing, flickering & ghosting
in & out. Python. Pythia. Python. Pythia.

I cry out, "Don't know what I'm supposed to do!"

She hisses, "*Non Plus Ultra*," as she expands her circle
into a large portal swirling, before me. She hisses.
I'm scared shitless. I take one step closer to the astral
zero of her, floating wormhole-like

unity

divinity   creation

destruction

Another cautious step towards her infinite loop,
towards the centre of her body, a gravitational
field even light could not escape. "Holy shite!"

I'm sucked into the centre of her portal
her inner outer space,
gateway

the infinite   of her mortal coil

no escape   feels safe survive   trust

her event horizon

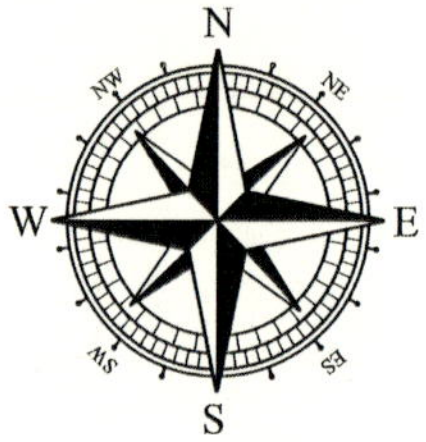

vortex

stretched by her tidal forces

noodle effect

ecstatic spaghettification

must look funny from the outside

Spinning in the psychedelic centre of Pythia's
circular entryway – maybe a stargate, no, snakegate.
Whoa!!! No magnetic north.

Fall with a ginormous splash into a limitless
sea *CRASH!* If I were an astrophysicist, I'd say
something's cosmologically wrong, not fishy.
Treading water again, aquaphobic flailing.

Above me, vertical cliffs on either side, possibly
the ancient Pillars of Hercules, somewhere in
the middle of the Straits of Gibraltar.

I remember Uncle Ed's old maps & according
to them this place should no longer exist. *So, where
the hell, am I?*

Smack dab in the middle of nothing, but ocean,
treading water, is where I am. Epic fail – the ultimate
flail. *The old sink or soar theory. We came from water
memory and to water memory we will return.*

In this world it seems I've got all the time in
the world ∵ time's slower here, more languid,
liquid. *Pop!* Asklepios appears beside me treading.
Lucky we're not marbles right now!

What a vision from the outside! Two miniscule
godheads bobbing in an endless sea of water,
we could be a couple of shipwreck survivors.

"Hello brother," I say, as I spit up a huge gulp
of salt water, "sorry."

His beard bends into a floating position in front
of him & he says, "two heads are better than one,
sister, here we are somewhere in the in-between."

Flicker. The lucid fish is on the blink *ZAP-ZAP*
experiencing transmission static – a disturbance
of two interlaced frames *ZAP* serious sci-fi vibe,
everything flickers in & out.

I oscillate between Hygieia & Rain. Asklepios
wavers between himself & someone else, who looks
like my doppleganger. What!? Who is she when
he's not Asklepios?

<<<<<<<*Che*>>>>>>>

"What!?" AsklepiChe smiles at both of me's.
No time to ask for details.

<<<<<<<no time to explain – just trust me>>>>>>>

"Okay." I go with the flow, let the ocean take me on the journey without judging. AsklepiChe lifts his/her hand, out of time, out of the water, it flickers in & out,

without missing a stroke, AsklepiChe whistles as if hailing a cab, which pings my funny bone, cracks me up *BLUB BLUB BLUB* "who's going to pick us up in the middle of oceanic nowhere?" Hilarious. Brain-shift. Fish autocorrect.

Everything's nacreous, mother-of-pearly. *Oops!* Overcorrect. Swing back. Reboot. Recoup.

Treading again, I snort a beaker of water, *nasal douche*, the very reason I don't like swimming. Crap! *CHOCKCOUGHBLURPBLURPBLURP* Default. I lift my head.

SNAP! What in creation's deviation?! "Damn!" Suddenly I'm eye-to-eye with a massive orphic hippocampus, or should I say, sea Dragon.

I jump out of my Hygieia skin, "Shite!"

In a low Dragonesque voice, the beast sooths me, "Don't be'est afraid. Ic eom þīn frēond. Ally, I am, friend."

"It wasn't me who whistled. It was my brother." I hork up a long string of snot, "Sorry," I blow my nose, "What language are you speaking?"

"Ophidinian."

"What?"

"A dialect of Reptilian."

"Oh."

"Yfel Atlas, êower ride, I am. Slîdan onto mîn back. Efstan. Make haste."

Quirky, somehow, I understand Ophidinian. Inconceivable. Whatever. At this point there's no point getting snagged on pesky details.

I swing my leg over the back of the beast, his Dragon scales amazingly silky against my skin.

Atlas opens his extraordinary, webbed wings & we fly off through the water as if it's the sky. Guess I accept the irrational when I'm totally freaked out, so I accept the absurd.

I make a quick glance backwards to AskChe, who yells, "you'll be safe with Atlas!"

Who's driving this dream anyway? Why am I here? And what's going on? Wonder how my real body's holding out in the easy chair?

We fly underwater, which is denser than air with caustic optics it's a wobbly underwater world filled with refraction distortions. Cool. Body torsion. Atlas blends with the blue green blue, green blue as we streak cyan through the ocean,

his physique glows opalescent, the light strobes,
we glide by, flying faster than the speed of light
0 to Mach 1, at Dragon speed. *[c]*

I grip his body tight with my legs as my fear
rages in a radiant frag

we whiz past a bed of coral
rising up from the depths

& I graze my toe on the tip
of the razor-sharp

coral skeleton, skreich
"Ouch!"

A single drop
of my blood falls

I see it
Atlas rears up

I look back

see the single drop

of my blood fall

through the cerulean

sea, everything pauses

then moves in slow mo

t
he
only
dot still
moving is
a single drop
of my blood – a
single drop of my
blood – falling thru
& into deepening blue
sea bluer than true blue
sea – a drop of me in slow
mo reverie – oh this blood
of life red blood of death
spinning to the bottom
the bottom of the
sea of me

unpause

Atlas growls, "weargbr¯æde drop,
you are un–l¯æd blôd."

Loose translation, 'a single drop of your blood.' Wonder what he's trying to tell me. *Decoding a fossilised enigma machine from the future.*

The earth rumbles, oh no, & the ocean roars, oh no
I've heard of underwater earthquakes, as it shakes
the redress is so great it swallows the sound of its
own seismic wave, "Holy frack! We're at the epicentre."

Hit by a jolt! Atlas growls, "weargbr¯æde drop,
you are un–l¯æd blôd."

Why am I continually fishing about blood?

Eclipsed, we fly thunder wave wild underwater
through the Strait of Gibraltar, *a heroine's deadly
arrow,* narrowly escaping catastrophe.

Besieged & bedraggled we land on the precarious
prow of the wraith ship, now the mere vestiges of
her former self, wrecked bone rack at the bottom
of the sandy sea.

On the edge, me & Atlas catch our breath & watch
the tempestuous shitstorm play out before our eyes.
We remain a safe distance from the disaster movie.

Wonder where Asklepios is. Reach down, touch my toe.
Ouch! *It stings with a burning sensation.* Wait, if I'm not
me whose toe am I touching & whose blood was shed?
Answer: Mine.

Doesn't matter, it hurts like hell. Ouch! Atlas is silent.
He's stoic, even regal, but grief-stricken. I want to say
something, but anything I say would sound trite.

Maybe we're sitting on top of sunken treasure. Maybe
there's something buried beneath us that might explain
our forgotten past – a clue to the human origin story
which is now lost to time, buried beneath the sea.

*Cracks in the earth emit gases, wonder if they're effecting
my thinking. I read somewhere that tube worms & clams –
love those methane gases as they bubble up – oh, & shrimp.*

Ripples of volcanic tremors rumbles, *drone base tone,*
which is unsettling sitting on top of eroding bones.
The ship graveyard erupts aghast as the earth shivers,
it shutters in a seismic wave of astonied aftershock,
quivering us equanimous.

In a sub-base voice Atlas whispers, "Nim þis mǣre, hit ne wyrð eft."

∵ ∴ Translated ∴ ∵
Take this great gift. It will not come again.

The rumble seems to originate in the middle of mega-waves, at the core of the nickel/iron earth, holy friggin...'

... pole reversal Pythia! Gotta get to back to Sweven. Hope they have bio-dome in place, with a radiation shield, yes! Holy kadoodle! Cataclysmic pole shift!

Death noodles! What the hell!? A pristine futuristic city rises out of the subterranean depths, from the bottom of the sea. Could be one of the wonders of the ancient world, lost to the sea at the end of the last ice age, or, the deluge. Maybe it sunk to preserve its own secrets. "Wow, this is totally quarked."

The city bursts forth from a lifeless state from below the seabed, awakening everything that's been asleep there – a spacey almost extraterrestrial real unreal world from the past & the future & the future of our alien past. It's all plastered together in a massive mythic pastiche – inconceivable – supernatural – the buried world rises. Opulent – breathtaking – beautiful. "Wowow!"

Skyscrapers built in spirals, release themselves from ancient ties Saturnalian & rise out from the depths of the sea inspired to be spires once more, maybe.

Atlas has tears in his eyes. He laments his lost home.

The towers resemble grand DNA strands rising up, soaring & winding around one other, serpentine into a receiving ocean of sky – a whole city of double

helixes rises fantastic as Neptunian erections through
bearing waters until they break the surface of the sea
way above & before us.

Rolling thunder, Dragon dice, pyramidal & spherical.
conal & symmetrical & geometrical & asymmetrical
faces & edges & vertices & cubes, they are

octahedrons & icosahedrons & tetrahedrons whirling
up in a trance, entranced,

they mesmerize & they hypnotize us,

marrying the living with the dead as they whirl up
out of the sands of time, they are

planets rising in ecstasy connecting the star light
of us to constellations in the night,

the moon sings & the sun rings & we are standing
on the threshold of the omnitemporal,

Atlas & me no longer exist, free of ourselves,
in unity, web weaving liquid silk.

"Omnia Ultra."

Notebook of LM

Entry XXVIII – Hidden Places

press spiral of tiny smooth coral shell, between
my finger and thumb – rub it, tingle sea swirl
back into memory – memory, rub it back into
memory,

the tiny shell touches me back in sensual echoes
of an opal past – chimerical, nacre pearl, amulet,

exuvia the size of a crescent moon, far enough
from far away, it is,

far from this day – it could be an exomoon
waxing the night sky day – to another galaxy,
coaxing me into her allure; I rub the iridescent
outline of her, you, Che,

the memory of pleasure pains me, but I return
home to her, again and again, for fear her silhouette
might leave me – leave me – Che, Che

I rub this tiny shell between my fingertips,
to take me back,

from this sphere to the first memento we ever
brought to this world from that, and O the knot
of that O-naut,

fishes me awake, awake, whimsy migrates
to the salty shores where we went without
leaving and we found so much more, O Che,

the tip of my tongue, recalls, the tip of your –
unsung, recollection of morning, that morning,

I woke to awaken your nipple, in Aitutaki
where we found this areola cochlea in the sand
the day before, remember – my woman, my man,

the way the oriola light, lit the flood current, breaking
against the shore, that sultry morning, high as island tide,

everything blurs together in a sideways glance
of glide – don't know why, can't place the order
of things now random, no chronology—

we rise with the sun, my tongue orbits a lunar
halo around the tip of your nipple, savory, swirling
saliva, twirling and trailing off, tail of Draconid,
we slip into a snake of almost awake, skin

side slide into island time-lapse zephyr, surrender
song from before it became a song, when it was
still someone's sweet epiphany, we sing,

to be sung one day by a chorus of celestial beings,
more leviathan than the world we live in, receiving
more than I could conceive, breathing an advanced
hymn in, in – elixir,

half-out, half-in of dream, dreaming a dream
without a dream – in and out of moiré reverie,

the tip of my tongue to the tip of your turritella,
light painting your pearl, long shudder speed,
until you whorl, infused in illusion of higher
gyres – deeper wilds,

I trace the ripples of your tempestuous sea, yes,
I follow you as you follow me, and O the flow
of my hula hands,

over the curves of your lands, free, where the rim
meets the sea at the golden hour of dawn, Che,
your hula-la-la-la upon, upon,

and into my hands, yes, wind around your neck
and up your spine, until your fiddlehead fern curls
and unfurls in a spiral of singing wildflowers, ziz,

we intertwine aril – aril of Yew, deepening red, fleshly
cup around the seeds of your eunoia, hibiscus, ahhhhh,

        this is not a memory about flowers,
        this is not a memory about loss,
        this is a release of pinned butterflies,
        ahhhhh,

your sounds a chorus of all the women who came
before you – us, singing, stringing frangipani along
long garland threads of untamed blossoms,

singing of breathing your red mango of ripened
hours into my omnitemporal heart beating
crimson, scry,

voices cry out from beyond – gender blending us
into deep song *PING* mouth immortal sings, well
of dreams & the jade pillow gates swing open

on many levels, in every realm, we meld worlds
quantum

reaching higher notes, beyond hearing, secret memos
bond to stormier maelstrom crescendos *PING*

the 9th chakra awakens, fire breathing Dragon
desire, connecting stars of Draco wyrd across
a cappella skies, scry,

morning archipelago, nowhere to arrive,

your sea splashes against my shores, as we slip
into the mix of constellations – twixt of fusion,
and a sprinkle of illusion, twisting thin sheets
into light rolling clouds,

all before the first rooster of morning crows
before we hear it almost out of earshot, listen,
listen as the sound as it makes its way all the way
around the island, and back again, it circles,

until there's no distance between it and us,
and the stars of last nights sky, deep inside,
deep inside each other's eyes,

your breath, your salt, déjà vu, déjà vécu,
déjà rêvé,

inside a slowly awakening day, over land and sea,
across the sky, arching, this time – a long stretch,
endless – breath inside breath,

the island awakens, plunging us into sweet
nothingness, the unquestioning of who we are,
and aren't, and who we might one day be,

we are beyond the body, beyond the mind,
woven into mentemotion, meta-emotion,

partaking in the song of many circles
superimposed on daybreak, nothing to
look for, nothing to find, or take, just

winding around water, wave swept up
and air, lightly blowing over our aroused
bodies, and trees, frangipani in a breath, wet
as the crowning hour, the crowing dawn,
in the wake of a flower, all levels of sound
going on, synthesize,

as tropical vines improvise so does our desire
intertwine, time, our O-nauts tie and untie
themselves cosmocosmical

<<<<<<<yes>>>>>>>

but not so far away that I can't taste you
in the arousal of this day, stringing me along
again, tethered to a tenuous thread of death,

<<<<<<<yes>>>>>>>

I trace the outline of you,

<<<<<<<yes>>>>>>>

shell between fingertips,

<<<<<<<yes>>>>>>>

sensing you senselessly,
still hopelessly in

yes.

Rain's Data Log
Private Notes XLV – Fish-a-thon

A fine revolution of irregular Platonic solids
rising & whirling & spiralling.

Could be Atlantis. No, can't be Atlantis,
the figment of a long lost imagineer.

Could've been built by giants.
No, but could be star-seeded
interdimensionality.

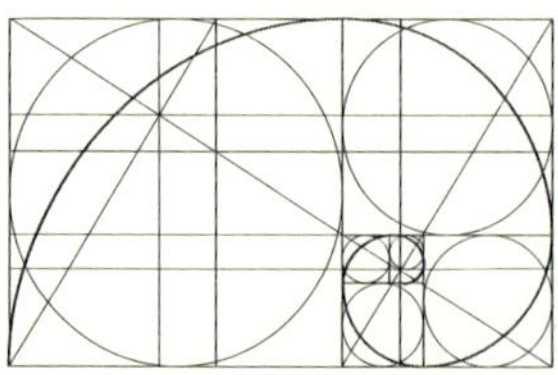

Hadean, zircon
intergalactic
marble.
No.
What I do know is,

the ancient futuristic city
has risen once more.

I turn to Atlas, say, "whose side am I on anyway?"

He winks, "on þǣre sīde of þurfan."

∵ ∴ Translated ∴ ∵
On the side of survival, otherwise, there're no sides."

He clears his throat, "n¯æfre," he shifts his weight.
Part of the prow crumbles beneath us & it slowly
descends to the depth. I lose balance in slow mo,
I grab him, to catch myself.

The deep-sea Dragon renews, "ðêos langlîce ono
tôcyme. Ah, dear heart f¯æle heortscræf this ðætte
couldn't sîn ûte êower happen with no you."

"I'm not in my right mind, right now. I'm not myself
I mean."

He ripostes, speaking with a thick dracontone
accent, "Heartache. Yes, you are not right as
you would be, Rain."

The moment distills. We take it in.

He adds, "æfterweard duguð speld afterward
the warrior plays fremian wægn stiell. Sê scêad
take wheels steal shadow, something, something,
destiny me bliss heart gân 3 êower save destiny."

"Thank you, Atlas," I say, "but it's a lot for me
to take in. I don't believe in fate." The wreckage
rumbles beneath our feet.

He roars over the rumble, "Seo stán þe is se Wīsra
stán, and se agent þæs weorc þāra wisa men, is
gehealden on þǣm afyllednesse eorðan."

My eyes glaze over like underwater donuts,
something, something, stone & the abyss of the earth.

Individually, we spiral into separate minds,
close enough to feel distant from one another.

We stare into the voidful world, destroying
itself, unsettled & struggling to right itself.

Atlas turns swiftly—

caught off guard, I grip his neck – he blasts
off underwater, Dragon torpedo headed in
the direction of our recent past, now altered.

His wide wings shimmer. They refract the light
aquiver – we stream through electric blue water
from abyssal to midnight through to twilight
& finally, the sunlight zone.

SNAP! We break the surface of the sea & climb
into the wide expanse of unfathomable sky.
The wind & the wet are at odds with one another,
whoa! A shiver.

Far, far below, the Island of Atlas rises skiffy.
We bank left in a wide arc over the vista orphic
which turns from terrain to topographic, vintage
mappa. *With so many views of the same thing,*
what exactly is change?

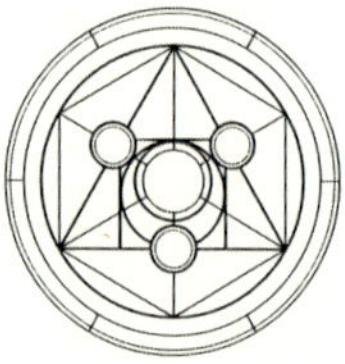

I morph into an esoteric cartographer & dub
the emerging map, 'tear from the eye of Atlas.'

Atlas ascends. We rise & we rise & we rise.

∵ ∴ Retrocausality ∴ ∵
Map monsters alive! Here be Dragons!

Below us the relief reveals a series of concentric
circles & these roundels rise out of the ground.

First, there are three distinct annuli of emerald-
green & then between them, three thinner rings
of red arise.

We level out, *almost like striking an equilibrium*
& for a moment I'm simply flying on the back
of a Dragon.

Wonder what's happening IRL? What's real life?
Where's Ask? Sometimes it's hard to tell what's
magical & what's macabre?

There're too many lives to calibrate at this point.
So I focus my attention on the circles within circles
below, red sea – green garden – red sea – green garden
rings.

They are.
What they are not.

Animated crop circles, hyperactive agriglyphs,
the ideations of extraterrestrials or cosmological
Platonic geometry.

And above us, shafts of golden rays are beaming
down from a ginormous orb – could be a sun-like
moon, or could be a moon-like sun.

Atlas navigates a broad sweeping reconnoiter
of the ethereal sky, the 360 levanter winds relax
me & I fall into the experience itself—

free of mind or even the thought of a thought.
I could be a bird – a bird soaring on the updraft
of a breeze through centuries, free—

PANSPERMIC PREPOSTULATION

Singularity from before the beginning.
I am compressed seedlessness,

living in nothingness, all that exists
are quantum fluctuations. Still flying
thoughts drift from other anchors.

In nonexistence, I'm hit by an extreme
energy, the birth of time & space. Arial
view of circular maze, labyrinth maybe
to Eidetic memory.

Hit by quarks combined with protons
& neutrons. The formation of light, voilà,

brought to life, the first star born to burn
in the fires fueled by nuclear fission.

Then there were more of me & the cosmic
entities became miniature life factories,
breeding like crazy.

But unfortunately, along with everything
except Immortal Jellyfish, we were destined
to turn supernova & KAPOW mature into
extremophile particle microbes floating in
outer space,

like tardigrades in a vacuum, we survived
radiation & we hitched a ride on the backs
of meteorites to travel to the blue marble
to combine with water, dust & gasses to
form new life.

Every element that makes up my body
was once part of a star, preposterous.

Must have zoned out into the pocket universe
of a pocket universe. Come to on the back
of a Dragon with no idea how long I've been riding.

He grumble-giggles. Think he's inside my head,
says, "Þær is nǣfre nān þing. Nāthing ne ārīsþ."

"But how does one thing become another?"

"Mæge þæt eall líf is," he dives down starting
a final landing sequence. His obvious aimpoint

is the nucleus of the circular grid, axis of which
is ringing, singing the music of the spheres.

We bank right, over the future of our advanced
past. Is there a word for a relic too advanced
for us to understand? *Obscurum reliquia.*

We land in the centre of the vestiges of what
was once a Grande Square, *luminosity blinding.*
Prismatic light reflects in psychedelic patterns
off the sheen of the white marble.

Atlas kneels with a regal bow which allows me
to smoothly slide onto the marble cobblestones,
sleek beneath my feet.

Bone-dry, I scan the strange new venerated land
for signs of life, for lost or wandering souls. But,
there is no one, nothing but the dead of silence.

Two worlds forte crash in my mind, cymbals strike
a climax in a finale. Can't remember when I missed
Gauge more – with such foresorrowed conscience –
yet I know he's right beside me.

I turn to face Atlas – his golden eyes tell me there
isn't much time – rush of sadness, still, I'm mesmerized.
Why have Dragons been so demonized, out-cast-away?
His irises twinkle with jewel-like glints & around
his almond eyes there is a radiance to his green
scales, an aura glow. His scales fit together tight,
which remind me of polished armor.

Likely the last of his kind, extinction & expansion
combined.

Using oculesic techniques, I speak with my eyes, expressing my deep appreciation.

Don't want this moment in altered adytum to end.

Try not to analysis, or even memorise, every detail, like I might at a birth or a death – I try to transcend the body & mind.

If I were a seer I would see—
Sea-foal heir. Dragon despair. Behemoth seahorse.

I would see—
Duality. Balance of creation & recreation, fertility & reproduction & what of destruction. I would see transformation. The Zeal Point of healing.

Hermetic sealing. *Hidden & forbidden knowledge.*
He winks at me.

I touch the star on his forehead, whisper, "As Rain, I'm running from the DOD,"

Smiling, his eyes still filled with sadness, he replies, "Þū mōst cēosan niwe wæge."

We remain suspended in *honorificabilitudinitatibus.*
I'm not a crier but I well up.

With a draco-whinny, he shutters his head slightly, releases a tooth & delivers it to me on the tail of fiery tendril from his mouth. *What's this?*

He switches to mind-speak, as now I can read him, *Dracontia, my dear,* he says, *it will assist you in seeing all times at once, so beware. Plant it just before war.*

Then he nudges me forth with his Dragon snout.
Ah ouch! The heat of his Dragon breath emanates
from his nostrils & singes my butt slightly.

Atlas snort-chortles Dragon-style, allowing me
a brief oculus into what he might have looked
like as a young Dragon.

Then he starts glitching, fragmenting pixelated,
I must return now, he laments, *HyRain, this world
was created by you & for you as a time sensitive crash
course glimpse into the world you are fighting to save.*

Sometimes I wish there was no such thing as time.
With noble poise & primeval deportment, he turns
to depart, leaving a trail of instructions, *for now,
locate point zero, think yourself where you want to be
& dive in.*

With that Atlas turns to stone, no, orichalcum.

"Wait," I cry, "Don't go. I need to know if you—"

XR! No long good-byes, in fact no byes at all.

I'm left stunned, in a state of extended shock.

I am.
I am not.

A sore thumb, sticking out, conspicuous as
an artificial flower in a field of ghost orchids.

The wind of the unknown world's spiralling,
it howls an elegy to a Dragon.

And I'm left in the centre of an empty square
on a vanished realm deserted as a plastic bag
caught in a garbage storm whizzing through
the gorge of a canyon, *ultraterrestrial ziggurat,*
holding the tooth of a misunderstood monster
between my fingertips.

Was it really my blood that triggered the fissure?
Suffering the aftermath of artificial existentialism.

I pace a zillion circles of sadness into the square.

Why did he say that? Where is this fish going?
Why isn't anything happening?

A tiny Ouroboros appears on the ground, moving.
It jumps up & grabs me. Atlas said, dive in. Unnerved,
I trust—

DIVE IN

to the small disk

headfirst down

Frig!

An intense light beam vector

shoots straight into me

close my eyes

one tick of time

on the clock of infinity, clicks

space junk debris

hurls past my head

the tooth brands the palm

of my hand

JUMP

I'm getting used to being spaghettified.

Hylomorphic Incantation

ᚨᛚᛚ ᚦᛁᛜᛊ ᚲᚺᚨᛜᛖ ᚹᛟᚱᛗ

The Willows form an inner circle
within the burning outer ring.
They are dressed in scarlet robes.

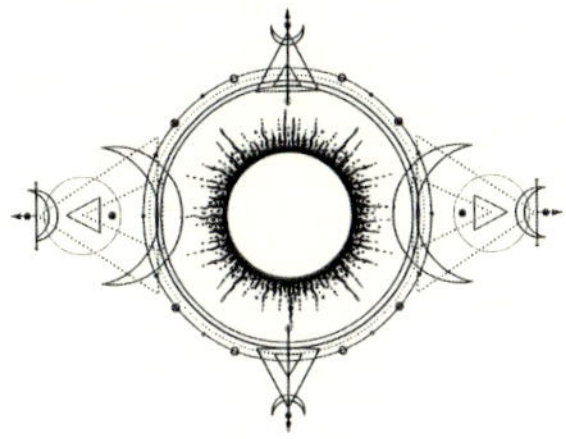

The elating darkness of night looms.
A wide circlet of fire burns around
the outer circumference of the clearing,
wild-eyed.

It is. It is nought.

Lily is suspended mid-air
horizontally,
at the centre of the Arcane Circle.

ΑΘΕ spins what appears to be a globe
within a globe within a globe
on the tip of her finger
above Lily's head.

It is. It is not.

A gordian knot spheroid.
The Willows watch in awe,
deep in not knowing,
what comes next.

(ΑΘΕ)
We enter the great mysterium,
spin, spin the recursion
of an impossible knot,
release via cosmic Reiki.
PING!

A bright coruscation shoots from the centre
of the spinning knot, centrifugal
it emanates gold light circumferentially,
and the glyph of the Arcane Circle
flare in gold lines of light.

(All)
Whirr-Williwaw-Whirr.
We will unknow all knowing
to know the unknown
until the web is sewn.

Nothing dies,
it just changes lives,
into another form.
Eudaimonia.

(ΑΘΕ)
Nothing ever came from nothing.
Spin, spin. Let eudaimonia begin.

Diegetic musica universalis harps in,
at Pleiades frequency. Lily's body moves in
waves of somatic awakening.

(All)
Yes-s-s-s-s-s-s!!!
Electric blue, as it is for you,
so be it for Rain and Gauge,

as they spin in and out
of eternity's
wheel.

(Jet)
We will bring them safely
home to Sweven.

ᛈᚨᛊᛏ ᛚᛁᚷᚺᛏᚾᛁᛜ ᛊᛏᛟᚱᛗᛊ
ᛁᛗᛊ ᛁᛗᛊ

δ θ γ

In spirit we go.

(3 claps in unison)

PING!

Rain's Data Log

Private Notes XLVI – All Thoughts on Deck

Open my eyes queasy. Sophie's sitting opposite me, with great urgency she snaps her fingers and spits, "you must leave, now!"

I leap out of my easy chair. "What?! No."

"Right now, and Gauge too. The DOD are smashing my door down upstairs!"

Gauge moves slowly, but stands. I ask, "How?"

"Visualize the ferry. Jump there in your mind."

"The ferry? What about Gauge."

"Yes, the ferry! You know the one. Don't question it, if you know it. Take Gauge's hand. You have the tools you need. Just do it. Imagine you're both there."

"Don't know if I can."

"You can. Trust yourself."

"What about you?"

"I'll fight them to buy you time, like in a reel scene scene. Now, close your eyes and go! Now!"

I take Gauge's hand; he nods as if to say you got this. I close my eyes. Think ferry. *JUMP*.

Gauge and I land mishmashed in the front seat of a car. I lighten the blow of our bodies entangled with, “Oops-a-daisy!” Never used that phrase before, awkward on all levels of awkward.

Traumatized. Too many fish jumps for one rogue scientist. Feel like I just graduated with a 4.0 GPA from the school of hard Nox! Mwahahaha! No! I think mad scientist is more apropos.

“Ouch, the hubcap’s gouging my hipbone.”

Gauge repositions himself in the passenger seat, mocking the hubcap as steering wheel, “Don’t worry, I got this. I knew this hubcap had a purpose.”

We half-laugh, roll our eyes.

I don’t understand time anymore. Have no idea how long we were at the Clay House. I redirect, “I hope Sophie is okay.”

He assures, “I think she’ll be fine, Rain, to answer your question, I think it’s sunrise.”

“Are you reading my mind?”

“I don’t know. Are you inside mine?”

“Haha! According to my calculations, this could be the first ferry which would put us at 6:00 AM ’ish.”

“Very precise.”

The morning light’s impressive, almost eldritch, but, something’s slightly off, somehow iffy. A quick scan tells me we’re the only car on the ship, which appears otherwise abandoned, bleak as a plutonium dead zone.

Gauge interrupts my assessment, "I'm starving."

"Me too," I say. Wonder what happened to Ruin.
Don't think the DOD is onboard, still I'm frazzled,
hyper-jittery compared to Gauge, cool as cryonics.

Sometimes I think my default is set to futility,
flummoxed I announce, "I'm going in search
of food. You wanna come?"

"Think I'll stay here, keep my eye on the car.
If you find food, bring some back for me.
You know what I like."

"Okay. Won't be long."

"If you don't return, where is our rendezvous?"

"Muster point? Why don't you just come with me?"

"Okay. Thought you'd never ask."

"But leave the hubcap here."

Moments later we're slinking around the ghost
ship like a couple of NPCs on a side-hustle, night-
mare, who's haunting who.

We dodge the prehistoric control cams and pin-
point a dead zone on the top deck where no one
can see us.

Gauge leans up against the bulkhead and points
his face to the sun. His skin turns gold. I don't know
how he came to be with me but, super glad he's here.
We both slip into stealth mode on separate isles.

I stand in complete stillness. Inhale. The gravity
of the situation invades me. I allow the sea air
to reorder my cells. Breathe in negative ions.

*The fragment of a flashback whizzes past my mind!
Holy crap, it's the residue of the Clay House fish. Dragon.
Atlas.*

*By shaking the DOD, we've likely triggered a full-scale
all-points Bureau-wide bulletin. Frick, we're officially
screwed.*

*<<<<<<<change your thinking – you manifest
everything you think>>>>>>>*

*Right. Is it possible I've normalized talking with
mind phantoms?*

Am I pretending to be someone I'm not? No, not.
418 I'm a teapot. In that case, I'm impersonating
my old self conforming.

The sea air churns in shades of a prophecy, gulls
cry out. Gauge is relaxed inside his own capsule.
Don't know how he does it. Won't disturb him.
He's really my touchstone, my brainiac lifeline.

*I'm suffering tech-withdrawal. I unplugged too fast.
I'm jonesing – the pinch, scroll, zoom, swipe, tap, double,
bane, boon, fame, death star flytrap – of my life.*

*Uncle Ed called it 'my refrain,' unwired for sound,
need a jab of matrix methadone. Miss Brainrot.*

*Clearly, I'm nothing without my phone, that's it,
I don't exist without screens and I need a hit.*

All the life rafts have been removed. Shite!
If we sink, I'm going to have to be Hygieia
and tread.

No, this is a real-world withdrawal meltdown.
I admit I'm a user, maybe even an over user,
but I was forced into digital detox cold turkey.

Wonder how Sophie is.

Wish I could call Mum to warn her. They've probably
got her bugged by now, or worse.

When this is over, I'm going to apologize bigtime.
I never understood what was going on until now.

Now I know why she never lived her life. I know why
she drowns herself in the deep end of shame every night.

It's a prolonged knee-jerk reaction to a life of oppression.
She desperately tries to bury her depression at the bottom
of the bottle. It's so hard to watch – to be around.

But I do know, the DOD's always utilized the fear
of familial retribution to keep dreamers in check.

The ethos of cenotaphs.

What blood type is she anyway? Maybe that's why,
oh no, holy crap, the dominos are starting to fall
into place.

My brother

might have the same— oh,

that's why Mum gave him— up,

she—

that's why she never

wanted to talk

about it.

Darknet!

I look up, "What the hell is that?"

Notebook of LM

Entry XXIX – The Scene of the Oneiro-crime

It is our first journey into Oneiro space together and it would 'naut' be our last.

That day I was aviatrix as we climbed the skies in our small single engine Cessna.

Over my headset I said, "don't take the dangers of flight or love for granted."

Quasi-confused Che half-laughed and I added, "I appoint you my official co-pilot."

She smirked, "I thought you'd never ask." Che knew I was flirting and she flirted back, not at all half-hearted.

We were pleasantly sardined in the tiny cockpit, flying into the narrow defile of a craggy canyon with mountains towering on both sides.

After navigating what seemed like a long tunnel we reached the opening on the other side, I yelled over the racket of the engine, "Look down. You wanna land on that abandoned airbase!"

Che yelled, "Nothing like landing in the middle of nowhere," and she gave a thumbs up.

BUMPBUMPBUMP my bad, from above the air-strip looked clear, but up close not so much. It's as rugged as the surface of Venus, 175. *THUMPTHUMPTHUMP*

I yelled, "Holy alligator cracks in the asphalt!
Sorry for the whiplash landing. I didn't know
Venus would be covered in impact craters!"

"It's okay, Lily," she chimed, "I just need a minute
to reassemble my brain."

After a brief respite sitting quietly in the cockpit,
we disembarked, shaken but not mixed, unfolding
our cramped legs, mermaids freed from a net, we
slowly regained our walking legs.

After a quick scan survey, I said, "we've landed on
the movie set of a horror film."

We mirrored one another, in a full 360° perusal
in unison, to take in the cataclysmic cacotopia.

In silent affirmation we agreed, there's something
sinister, almost diabolical, about this derelict place.
Straightforward, it's haunted.

I added, "Let's get out of here before the zombie
apocalypse kicks in."

Che concurred, "It's definitely a nightmare,"
and we sprang into action.

SHHHH in my haste to escape the creepy outpost
I flooded the airplane engine.

But still I rushed to the nose of the plane
and pulled the screw propeller down *SHHHH*.

Even in a fish, a flooded engine causes
the propeller to kick back and *SHHWHACK!*

One of the blades caught my hand
with a *SHHWHACK* so violent

it threw me back on the ground.

I tucked and I rolled back on the tarmac,
away from the plane, in the fetal position
screaming !@#$%^-$%^&*%!!

Che jumped out of the co-pilot seat to help me.
By that time I was on the ground screaming bloody
murder.

I looked up at her. She used her body to block
the sun from my eyes. She said, "hold on, baby,
stay with me."

Lightning speed I had a wisecrack comeback,
"I'm still alive for fucks sake! I'm going to live."
We laughed despite the fix.

We tried to jump, but were stuck in the fish
for reasons we would come to realize later.

I looked down and I still had a thumb, but it
was hanging off my left hand, like a dead haddock.

Woozy. The moment I saw it I passed out,
and when I came to, I was in Che's arms, looking
into her eyes close up.

And it was there, smack dab in the middle
of nothing, but a bad situation,

that she leaned down and kissed me
on the lips. Our first kiss,

I forgot my thumb and acquiesced amorous,
profoundly aroused.

Time magnified as it does in an accident.

I can still feel her kiss through the memory.

Next, we're standing beside on a deserted
gravel road which ran parallel to the airstrip.
I said, "Let's thumb!" as a joke, on a dirt road.
Then I felt myself turn pale. Che caught me.

No idea how much time passed, sliding in
and out of consciousness. Finally, an old jalopy
hiccupped up beside us and it stopped.

A disembodied voice with a hillbilly accent
asked, "You need *sum* help neighbors?" *TWANG.*

Without thinking, we slid into the backseat, and
in a blink we were at 'Emerg.' The 'Emerg' sign
was handwritten in red paint, which was scary
even in my delirium. I stuttered to the driver,
"Thanks for the lift. Adieu." And I staggered out.

The old wizard shot me a toothless smile, his eyes
filled with compassion – on our side. 'Emerg' was
an outpost hospital mirage with no waiting room.
Go fish.

I was immediately admitted, and they assisted me
to lie down. The gurney bed was in a curtained cubicle.
I was there for at least ten seconds before Doctor
Feelgood swept into the shrouded room. Maybe
it was the agony – she looked like an apparition
en route to a poltergeist party.

She touched my hand. I spiked in pain, "Ow!"
Feelgood bit back, "Don't be such a cry baby!"

To test her, I shot her a zero-tolerance leer, and
said, "Vocatus atque non vocatus, Deus aderit!"

Feelgood got the joke and winked at me in code,
which was a good sign 'cause it told us she's not
a spy or a DOD useful idiot!

Ice broken, we were on operation super fast-track.
Feelgood put my thumb in a splint and gave me some
"killer painkillers." They were oblong with 144000
inscribed on their side.

She handed Che a ring and said, "Intel tells us
you've been made, so take this finger grenade.
If you need to obliterate the safety is the amber
stone. Just pull it, count three, and bazinga
blitz."

Che said, "Sapph-fire away! Thanks, we have
to run now, to make it back to zero."

Feelgood nodded, exclaiming, "Hurry," Already
high, I slurred, "Adieu."

Che and I raced counter-wise back to the plane
in an ambulance. Emergency taxi. From there, we ran
across the remaining tarmac and jumped in the Cessna

cockpit ready to take-off. Che and I stole a terrified
glance to one another, as a huge militia of DOD
Agents advanced. They poured out of the dilapidated
hangers like well-armed roaches.

(((((((security alert)))))))

The zombie creepers rushed towards us in black tactical gear with exoskeletons for max protection, not ours.

Also closing in, an endless wave of bipedal humanoid robots carrying dual FN F2000's.

(((((((security alert)))))))

Great! A robotron army of clone drones – zoned out, disconnected from reality – controlled remote control, literally flooded the broken strip. Stoned as a spice addict I shouted to Che, "The future's now!" Then I gunned the Cessna and we began to taxi toward takeoff.

(((((((security alert)))))))

Bellicose agents blasted shoot-and-point red-laser guns at our puny timeworn craft. I noted aloud, "By Troth! They're coming in hot!" They executed a hostile assault pummelling our plane with bullets, but not debilitating us. We hit the sky flying sideways, in a wonky ascent.

I yelled, "Mayday Che! I'm higher than an albatross."

Che hollered, "Let's deep-six these fuckers!" She slid the Feelgood ring off her thumb, pulled the amber pin and tossed it out the window,
three
    two
        one
            bazinga, it exploded midair,

between us and the DOD hostiles, the stars aligned.

A tempest fire shitstorm split the sky in two, and
our tiny craft tremor-warped, flea in a windstorm.

We annihilated the entire army of Agents and bots
in a magnificent pyrotechnic spectacle, I shouted,
"We're officially abscotchalaters," then I turned
our Cessna on her nose
          high as the blue star of Icarus
                    and we fled in the direction of zero.

The perks of a 144000, besides losing the feeling
in your face – is, all separations become erased like
those between mouth and mind, out-of-body

experience. I was watching myself from the outside –
immersed in the radical lucid riff of an addled brain,

I spoke into my headset, "I am not a plane, I'm a giant
blue morpho butterfly with enormous wings, morpho
blue, colors wink in and out, I spread my wings into
the cartoon clear blue sky, miraculous!

Morpho butterfly eggs change colors to protect them-
selves too, true.

Blue, my butterfly wings metamorphose in the late
afternoon light – they wink iridescent, blue butterfly
wings – mother-of-pearl twinkle – they're crystals
blinging in sunlight – peacock blue butterfly wings,

of abalone – light as air – my pinions stretch out
in suspended animation – fearless flares – bright
blue flames of morpho alchemy – my wingtips
skim the peaks of mountaintops for me."

Che roared back, "you got this, blue butterfly."

"Allow me to grant you a wish."

Full of fake confidence, she yelled, "I can't find
us on the map! Don't know where we are! Lost,
to the mountains. They all look the same from
up here. And there's no one to ask where we are,
there are no service stations to ask for directions!"

I rallied, "If I wasn't high on horse tranq's
I'd be completely freaked out."

"All our markers have been erased so we can't
be traced which means we're hooped. If anything
happens to you, who's going to land this butterfly?"

"You might have to take a crash course."

We got giddy but I added, "I can guarantee you,
after we smoked those Agents, our names were
added on the top of the Most Wanted list!"

"You ARE the most wanted! And for all it's worth,
I trust you."

"A blue morpho butterfly?"

"Better to trust a butterfly than a human!
Bottom line, this is electrifying. I feel alive."

"Keep your eyes peeled for DOD nets and traps!
We don't want to end up pinned in a butterfly
collection!"

Che makes an about-face. "Change our thinking.
Listen to intuition."

"I'm lapping up your clichés like a ravenous cat!"

We screech! Just before I derail – my mind jangles

loose,
wings of butterfly

dust particles in sunbeams

bends into blue metallic glimmer

blue Pleiades sensorial
blue

tastebuds on my butterfly feet

tasting
the sky
twinkle-
toes

incandescent sky blue

elderflower soles

blue savor sky flower jasmine

vapour mist clouds

Che if fish could fly

sky high I would

A E A E A E

O P E N I

N G S K Y

molecules of me change

as be fore

an earth quake

Che preferred the word

hermaphrodite

to inter

sex

fish you

Rain's Data Log

Private Notes XLVII – Playing with a Full Deck

But what's that? *Darknet!* The entire ship, the ocean, birds and the sky, are travelling inside a giant Ovoid. Talk about a ship in a bottle.

Just accept and move on. Best strategy – deal with things as they arise. Right! Take in the sun.

DEEPERREM

FISHING AROUND

Pons, pons are pinging, phantoms in caves are zinging around star-like, shooting across the anterior prefrontal cortex of my brain. Sleight of eyesight, pons are pinging,

zinging, flickering, snapping my synapses, signalling. Its an outer space lightshow – fireworks, fireballs, shooting stars – on deck, in my mind, inside a giant O dome.

The Oneironaut appears in the stars wearing aviatrix gear, holding a red umbrella, as protection from the pon shower. She's attached to an umbilical cord,

space tether

safety line

tow rope

lifeline.

Her long green hair, strands of her long green hair extend from her vintage pilot cap with flaps. She's clad in a bomber jacket & goggles. *What are you doing here?* She doesn't answer.

Beside O is my doppelganger, only less tomboy than me,
a lot more girly. She says,

<<<<<<<*hi, i'm Che, Lily's wife*>>>>>>>

I ask, "who's Lily?"

<<<<<<<*my wife – the Oneironaut*>>>>>>>

"Double oh. I didn't know she was married."

<<<<<<<*think about parabolic orbit*>>>>>>>

"$C_3 = 0$ orbit"

<<<<<<<*yes – one direction to escape
the other to be captured*>>>>>>>

Notebook of LM

Entry XXX – Flying High

My mind lands back in the cockpit. The only sound is air whistling. The sound of the plane is gone, all I hear are ghosts, the whispers of ghosts.

I made it back to my first memory of—

Sin-eaters say, first you feel the force field surround you. Then the atmosphere changes as you approach the outer edges of a sacred grove of Oaks. They say, you must pass through that wall of energy to reach the teachings of the holy grove, the ogham lifeforce.

Wonder if Che feels the contact high. Look over to her in silence and for the first time I click into pure instinct.

The entire magnetic field is superimposed, visible power grid, on the sky before us.

All paths of all the butterflies who ever flew that sky appeared before us, in neon blue lines – all butterfly flight patterns. I fly inside the magnetic force field of an altered sky, as myself and blue Morpho butterfly combined.

Even high I intuit where we are, and where we're going, without knowing or not knowing.

Flying for flying's sake, in the trust of nought knowing where we are or where we aren't, in the unknown of unknowing, feeling my way by my wilds

in the space

in between space which

separates incorporates

hypnagogia hypnopompia

transitory stationary

half in half out

twilight seeing

between birth death

there is but one breath

my only wish is to be with Che
PING

the moment two people see one another
as themselves, becomes the twinkling
that binds them and carries them
through all darknesses *PING*

When we finally made it back
to zero – zero no longer existed,

but together we found our way
back to Sweven,

in the darkness our hands
had found one another,

mine broken,
she helped me heal,

Che told me she was ambiguous.

I told her she was lucid,
and I would love every aspect
of her,

for real.

Rain's Data Log

Private Notes XLVIII – The Real Leap

The stories we tell ourselves, are seldom
the stories we tell others. The wind blows
my hair.

To fish or nought to fish, that is the question.
The good news is – I can fish – that's clear.
Did I manifested this?

Yes, it was me. Wow. I made us jump here,
myself. *Was it myself?* No. *Yes, it was myself.* Wow.
This is a lot to take in.

And I was able to bring Gauge. He's really
loving the ocean. Won't tell him it's not real.
Does it matter? I love this sea air. We must
be Tardigrades to survive.

Why do I keep thinking of Uncle Ed? Maybe
he's still alive. *No nought. Is he still alive?*

My intuition is telling me he is. The Bermuda
Triangle story always sounded sketchy.

I'm experiencing panic-ation nausea, seeing
exploding stars and spherical swirls. Living inside
the optical illusion of a surrealist painting. *Yeah,
inside a surrealist painting, looking out at myself looking
in at myself.* Why am I thinking about art?
I never think about art.

Stop stalling! Grab Gauge's hand and *JUMP.*

Notebook of LM

Entry XXXI – Flowerdogs

Somehow the Willows were able to tear down
the wall and allow me to see in.

Today, I feel changed. My wounds are a little
further away – almost as if I am on the verge
of fishing. I can feel it!

The animals close in around me, feather and fur,
fish and foul. Nuance divebombs me and lands
with a *SQUAWK*. Ajax, peacock howls outside,
presses his fan against the glass. They all know
something's up.

Several hours pass. I remain frozen in distilled
time – not doing anything, not even thinking.
I hold onto hope. Don't want to lose my grip.

Hit the wall. Slide. Crash. Die. Pick myself up
off the ground. Repeat. Break the cycle. Done.

There's a scratching at the door. It's Shumba
and Violet. They must've been out all night.
They're filthy.

I spritz them down. A river of mud and flowers
flow from their bodies and feet in a river of cherry
blossom petals.

Violet, my flowerdog, shimmies. I inner titter
with sounds non-human, funny that. She looks
me square in the eye, free of mystery, and smiles.

Shumba, my cherry blossom love, cants his head.
Rivers of spring flowers circle the drain, before
they disappear,

reminds me, of the snake who eats her own tail,
and the real adventure ends as it begins.

Fini Ø2

To be continued in Ø3...

ACKNOWLEDGEMENT

I acknowledge the Indigenous Peoples and extend my respect to the Elders and Knowledge Holders, past and present, who have been stewards of this land.

A resounding thank you to publisher Brad Morden for believing in this project from its genesis. His encouragement is integral at every turn, shaping segues as they unfold. Together, we assemble this vast cosmological puzzle.

Galaxies of gratitude to my editor, Dr. Micheline Maylor, for her sharp eye and divinely insightful guidance. She believes in me and the process, inspiring me at every step and sharing a passion for telling this story with as much fervor as I do. Blessed be.

The brilliant poet and educator Billeh Nickerson was also integral to this journey, and I am grateful for his continual ruminations and illuminations – with grace.

Thank you to Leesha Withrow, a trusted reader since day one, Carol Dale for her proof-reading prowess and to Patrick Crean for his ongoing council. I am forever grateful to Andrew Forbes for his patience and steady hand in all thing's techno, and to Michal Kozlowski for bringing the interior of this book to life with artistry and precision.

Lastly, thanks to Courtney Bell, Stephen Donahue, Martin Guderna, Malcolm Mooney, Sally Ogis, Michael Roberts, Gabrielle Rose, Michèle Stanners, Jo Steffens, Johnny Trinh, Mark Williams & Maralyn Wilson for their love and support. Heartfelt thanks to all my friends for understanding as I disappeared from this world into the hyperverse of this book.

I appreciate all who read *The ONEIRONAUT*, and thank you for your marvelous missives, which echo as if from a shared fish.

Photo: Kimberley French

Sheri-D Wilson is a prolific author of 15 books of poetry. She's authored 3 produced plays, created 4 short films and produced 3 word & music albums.

Known for her captivating reading style, her work has received many awards and honours, including the Order of Canada, an honorary Doctor of Letters – Honoris Causa from Kwantlen University, Poet Laureate Emeritus of Calgary, the Stephan G. Stephansson Award for Poetry, and the Women of Vision Award. Her lifework has always centered around creating space for others to share their voices and fostering a broader sense of community.

She splits her time between Calgary & Vancouver, with her dog Willow.

www.sheridwilson.com
insta @sheridwilson
twitter @SheriDWilson
facebook.com/facethepoet